AF521939

INDIA—Transplanting young rice shoots in muddy field.

# Rice

by
**Coleen and Bob Simmons**

Illustrated by **Mike Nelson**

A Nitty Gritty Book*
Published by
Nitty Gritty Productions
P.O. Box 5457
Concord, California 94524

*Nitty Gritty Books—Trademark
Owned by Nitty Gritty Productions
Concord, California

ISBN 0-911954-49-X
Library of Congress Catalog Card Number: 78-71487

# TABLE OF CONTENTS

INDIA—Workers bring in the sheaves.

# RICE

Rice is believed to have been cultivated for more than 7,000 years and to over half of the world's population it is an essential part of the daily diet. Varieties have been developed which are well adapted to many soils and climates, making it possible to grow rice in most tropical and semi-tropical regions.

Rice by itself is a bland, neutral food, making it a perfect companion for a variety of spicy, pungent or sweet accompaniments. Rice is so adaptable that it can be served as part of any course in a meal—appetizer, soup, salad, main course and dessert.

There are several varieties of rice available.

**Long grain** is the most commonly used rice. The grains are three to four times as long as they are wide. Cooked grains are not sticky and rice is fluffy. This is the type of rice generally preferred in the Middle East and in India where some of the world's highest quality rices are grown. These are sometimes available in specialty shops and are called Persian or Basmati rice.

**Converted or parboiled** rice is long grain rice that has been specially processed to retain natural vitamins. Converted rice needs more water and a longer cooking time.

**Medium and short grain rice** — Grains are round or almost round. Cooked grains absorb more water and tend to stick together. This is the rice generally preferred by Japanese and Italian cooks. It is used for risottos, molded dishes and desserts.

**Brown rice, long or medium grain** — This rice has had only the hull removed. The bran and germ are retained, giving brown rice a chewy nut-like character. Brown rice needs more cooking time and more liquid than white rice.

**Wild rice** is not rice at all, but is an aquatic grass seed, harvested by hand. It has a unique nutty flavor and chewy texture. Wild rice goes well with roasts or chicken and can be combined with plain long grain rice to make a more reasonably priced dish.

**Precooked or instant rice** is rice that has been precooked and dehydrated to reduce cooking time. Because the texture and flavor are not as satisfactory as freshly cooked or reheated regular rice, precooked rice is recommended only when time is critical.

The following recipes will indicate special cooking methods for the rice if it makes a difference in the dish. Otherwise follow the package instructions. A basic formula is two cups of liquid for one cup of uncooked rice. The rice is cooked in a tightly covered saucepan undisturbed until all the liquid is absorbed and the grains are tender. The cooking time depends on the kind of rice.

Most rice available in the market today does not need to be washed. In fact, the water will wash away vitamins and minerals. Exceptions are Persian and Indian (Basmati) rices which aren't well washed before packaging, and Japanese rice, which is coated with talc or starch and should be washed in several changes of water until the water runs clear.

Rice is delicious cooked in chicken stock or beef broth. For salads, it can be cooked in orange or lemon juice, and for Mexican style rice, tomato juice may be used.

Cooked rice will keep in the refrigerator for at least a week. It should be kept tightly covered or it will absorb other flavors.

Rice freezes well either in a tightly covered container or in a boilable pouch which can be defrosted with a minimum of further cooking of the rice.

Uncooked rice will keep almost indefinitely if it is in an air tight container in a cool dry place. Indeed, some Indians believe that polished rice improves if aged two to three years before cooking. Brown rice, because it contains the germ, is more perishable and should be refrigerated if it is to be kept for longer than a few months.

We hope you will enjoy these recipes and gain some new ideas of your own for cooking with rice.

INDIA—A farmer using bullocks to thresh rice grains from stalks.

# APPETIZERS, SOUPS AND SALADS

Rice is excellent in appetizers and salads because it blends so well with herbs, vegetables and flavorful bits of sausage or seafood. Most of these recipes use cooked rice so if you have some left from another meal, use it to create a delicious appetizer or a salad.

Try hot curried cheese balls or sausage stuffed peppers for a savory accompaniment to cocktails. Clams stuffed with brown rice or the green chile soup are imaginative starters for a dinner party.

The rice salads are best made ahead so the flavors have a chance to blend. They are especially nice for a luncheon or picnic.

These recipes are only a starting point. Use them as basic ideas for your own creations with your family's favorite ingredients.

# STUFFED CLAMS

Fill clam shells with this tasty brown rice, garlic and clam mixture. Serve hot for a first course.

1 can (6-1/2 ozs.) chopped clams
2 tbs. butter
3 green onions, minced
2 cloves garlic, minced
1 tbs. flour
1/2 cup cooked brown rice
1/4 cup parsley, finely chopped
18 clam shells
1/2 cup fresh bread crumbs

Drain clams and reserve juice. Melt 1 tablespoon butter in small saucepan. Saute onions and garlic until soft, 2 to 3 minutes. Stir in flour, cook another minute. Add clam juice. Cook until sauce thickens. Stir in brown rice, chopped clams and parsley. Fill clam shells with mixture and place in individual baking dishes filled with rock salt or dried beans to keep shells from tipping. Melt remaining butter in small skillet. Add fresh bread crumbs and saute until lightly browned. Place bread crumbs on top of clam mixture. Bake in a 400°F. oven 10 to 15 minutes until very hot. Makes 6 servings.

# STUFFED PEPPER APPETIZERS

Use small peppers about 2 inches long for this recipe.

2 link sausages
8 fresh green chile peppers
1 tsp. salt
1 tbs. vinegar
1 tbs. butter
4 green onions, thinly sliced
1 small clove garlic, minced
1/2 cup cooked long grain rice
1 egg white
Parmesan cheese

Cook and finely chop sausages. Cut peppers in half lengthwise, leaving stem on. Scoop out seeds and membrane with spoon. Fill small saucepan with water. Add salt and vinegar. Parboil peppers for approximately 5 minutes. Drain and let cool. Melt butter in small skillet. Saute green onions and garlic until soft. Stir in sausages and rice. Cook for another minute or two. Beat egg white with fork and fold into rice mixture. Stuff each pepper half with rice. Place on oiled, ovenproof serving platter or baking dish. Sprinkle with Parmesan cheese. Bake in 350°F. oven 10 minutes, or place under broiler until lightly browned and hot. Makes 16 appetizers.

# CURRIED RICE AND CHEESE APPETIZERS

These cheese balls make a great hot, creamy accompaniment to drinks. They can also be made with minced clams or green chiles.

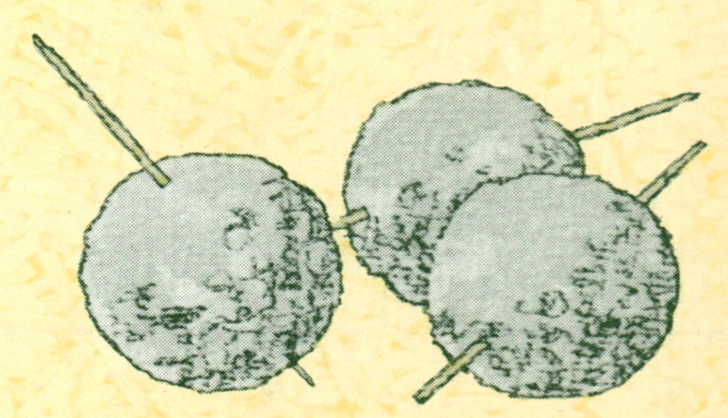

2 tbs. butter
1/4 tsp. curry powder
2 tbs. flour
1/2 cup milk
1/2 cup grated sharp cheese
1/4 cup Parmesan cheese
1/4 tsp. **each** white pepper and dry mustard
3 to 4 drops Tabasco
1 cup cooked rice
1 egg, beaten lightly
cracker crumbs
oil for deep frying

Melt butter in small saucepan. Add curry powder and cook 1 minute. Stir in flour and cook 2 minutes. Gradually add milk and cook, stirring, until sauce is very thick. Mix in sharp cheese, Parmesan, pepper, mustard, Tabasco and rice. Drop teaspoonfuls of rice mixture onto a large plate. Refrigerate 1 to 2 hours. When well chilled form into small balls. Dip into beaten egg and then into cracker crumbs. Heat oil to 375°F. Fry rice balls a few at a time until lightly browned. Drain on paper towels. Serve immediately. Makes 20 appetizers.

**Variations**

Green Chile and Cheese — Omit curry powder. Add 4 tablespoons chopped green chiles and 2 green onions thinly sliced to butter before adding flour.

Hot Clam Appetizers — Omit curry powder. Mince 1 clove garlic and add to butter before adding flour. Drain 1 can (6-1/2 ozs.) minced clams. Fold into sauce with rice.

# DOLMAS

Stuffed grape leaves are suitable for party appetizers or picnics.

1/4 cup olive oil
1 large onion, chopped
1 clove garlic, minced
1/2 tsp. salt
1/4 tsp. pepper
1/2 cup uncooked rice
1/2 tsp. dill weed
3 tbs. minced parsley
2 tbs. chopped almonds or pine nuts
1/4 cup lemon juice
1/2 cup water
3 tbs. olive oil
1/2 lb. mushrooms, finely chopped
1 jar (8 ozs.) grape leaves in brine
2 tbs. olive oil
2 tbs. lemon juice
1-1/2 cups water or chicken stock

Heat 1/4 cup olive oil in large skillet. Add chopped onion and garlic. Saute until tender but not browned. Add salt, pepper and rice to onions. Cook slowly 10 minutes, stirring frequently. Add dill, parsley, nuts, lemon juice and water. Stir well. Cover and simmer gently until liquid has been absorbed, approximately 15 to 20 minutes. Heat 3 tablespoons olive oil in another small skillet. Saute chopped mushrooms for 3 to 4 minutes until mixture is fairly dry. Add to rice mixture after rice has cooked. Rinse grape leaves under running water. Separate, and trim the long stems. Place leaves shiny side down on a plate or board. To fill, place 1 teaspoon of rice mushroom mixture near the stem end and roll up jelly roll fashion, tucking in the sides of the leaves to make a neat package as you roll. Place stuffed leaves in a skillet large enough to hold them in one layer. Pour in olive oil, lemon juice and water. There should be enough liquid in pan to come half-way up the sides of the dolmas. Place a large flat lid or plate directly on top of rolls. Cover pan with foil or another lid. Simmer 35 minutes. Add more water during cooking if necessary. Remove to a platter and cool. Makes approximately 25 to 30 dolmas.

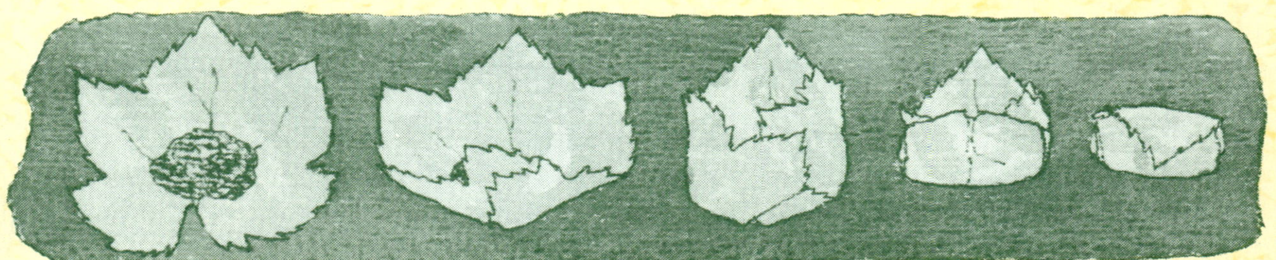

INDIA—A farmer sells his rice in the open-air market.

# GREEN CHILE AND RICE SOUP

Creamy and mildly spicy this elegant first course soup will please your dinner guests.

1 tbs. butter
6 green onions, thinly sliced
1 can (4 ozs.) green chiles
2 tbs. dry sherry
1-1/2 cups chicken broth
1/2 tsp. salt
1/4 tsp. white pepper
1/2 cup finely diced ham or cooked chicken
1 cup cooked rice
1 cup light cream
cilantro leaves or chopped pimiento

Heat butter in small skillet. Saute onions until soft. Drain green chiles and remove seeds. Place sherry, chiles and cooked onions in blender container. Blend until mixture is smooth. Bring chicken stock to boil in a medium saucepan. Add blended mixture, salt, pepper, diced meat and rice. Cook uncovered 10 minutes. Add cream and heat for another minute. Garnish with cilantro leaves or pimiento. Makes 4 servings.

# SHRIMP AND RICE SOUP

1/2 lb. small uncooked shrimp in shell
2 tbs. oil
1/2 cup chopped celery
1 medium onion, chopped
1 large clove garlic, minced
1-1/2 cups tomato or V-8 juice
1 can (14 ozs.) chicken broth
1 bottle (8 ozs.) clam juice
2 cups water
1/8 tsp. cayenne
1/4 tsp. ground coriander
1 tsp. salt
2 cups cooked rice
1 tbs. lime juice
fresh cilantro and chives for garnish

Shell and devein shrimp, reserve shells. Heat oil in large saucepan. Saute celery, onion and garlic until soft. Add shrimp shells and saute for 3 to 4 minutes. Add tomato juice, chicken broth, clam juice, water, cayenne, coriander and salt. Bring to boil. Simmer covered 25 to 30 minutes. Strain broth and return to saucepan. Discard vegetables and shrimp shells. Add cooked rice and shrimp. Simmer 4 to 5 minutes until shrimp are pink and soup is hot. Add lime juice. Ladle into serving bowls. Garnish with cilantro and chives. Makes 6 servings.

# COLD LEMON SOUP

Serve this soup in pretty glass bowls, garnished with thin lemon slices.

6 cups chicken broth
1/3 cup uncooked rice
1 tsp. salt
3 eggs
1/3 cup lemon juice
1 lemon, thinly sliced

Combine chicken broth, rice and salt in saucepan. Bring to boil. Cover and simmer until rice is tender, approximately 15 minutes. Remove from heat. Beat eggs in a separate bowl until pale yellow. Slowly beat in lemon juice. Carefully stir some of the hot broth into egg-lemon mixture, beating continuously. Add egg-lemon mixture to rest of broth. Cool and refrigerate. Serve very cold with one or two lemon slices as garnish for each serving. Thickness of soup will depend on richness of chicken broth. Stir well before ladling into serving dishes. Makes 6 servings.

# CARROT RICE SALAD

1 avocado
2 cups grated raw carrots
1 cup cooked rice
1/3 cup pine nuts
2 tbs. lemon juice
1 tbs. wine vinegar
1/3 cup olive oil
1/4 tsp. **each** sugar and white pepper
1/2 tsp. salt
black olives or parsley for garnish

Peel avocado and cut into small cubes. Combine with carrots, rice and pine nuts in serving bowl. Mix together lemon juice, vinegar, olive oil, sugar, pepper and salt in small jar. Shake well and pour over carrot mixture. Toss gently with fork. Garnish with black olives or parsley sprigs. Makes 4 servings.

**Variation** — Segmented orange slices or diced apple may be added to carrot salad in addition to above ingredients.

# SUMMER PICNIC SALAD

This goes well with barbecued hamburgers, hot dogs or steaks.

3 cups cooked rice
1/3 cup finely chopped mild onion
1/2 cup chopped sweet pickles
3 hard-cooked eggs, chopped
1/4 tsp. salt
1/4 tsp. white pepper
1/4 tsp. celery salt
2 tbs. mustard
1/2 cup mayonnaise
1/2 cup sour cream
1 tbs. pickle juice
1 tsp. Worcestershire sauce

Combine all ingredients in a large mixing bowl. Toss with two forks until well mixed. Makes 6 servings.

# COLD SHRIMP AND RICE SALAD

1/2 cup uncooked rice
1 cup chicken broth
1/2 tsp. salt
2 tbs. white wine vinegar
2 tbs. lemon juice
3 tbs. olive oil
3 tbs. finely chopped walnuts
3 tbs. finely chopped celery
1 tbs. finely chopped green peppers
2 tbs. finely chopped black olives
2 tbs. finely chopped parsley
1 tsp. onion juice or grated onion
1/3 lb. cooked small shrimp
1/4 tsp. dried tarragon

Cook rice in boiling chicken broth 15 to 20 minutes until tender. Let cool slightly and add salt, wine vinegar, 1 tablespoon lemon juice and 2 tablespoons oil. Toss lightly with a fork. Add walnuts, celery, green pepper, olives, parsley and onion juice. Cover and chill for several hours. Combine cooked shrimp, remaining oil and lemon juice, and tarragon in separate bowl. Cover and chill. Just before serving combine shrimp with rice salad and serve on lettuce leaves, or if preferred, mound rice salad in center of salad plate and garnish with the shrimp and more black olives. Makes 4 appetizer servings.

# TUNA RICE SALAD

Surround this salad with sliced cold meats and cheese for a light supper, or fill ripe tomato halves with the salad mixture and serve for a first course.

1 can (6-1/2 ozs.) tuna
2 cups cooked rice
1 cup cooked peas
1 cup diced Swiss cheese
2 tbs. parsley, chopped

2/3 cup mayonnaise
1 tsp. anchovy paste
1/2 tsp. dry mustard
2 tsp. white wine vinegar
1/4 tsp. white pepper

Drain and flake tuna. Combine with rice, peas, cheese and parsley. Toss lightly with a fork. Combine mayonnaise, anchovy paste, dry mustard, wine vinegar and pepper. Mix well and add to rice mixture, stirring just enough to combine ingredients. Makes 4 side dish servings, or fills 6 large tomato halves.

U.S.A.—Planting rice by biplane in Louisiana.

# ENTREES

Throughout the world almost every cuisine has special dishes made with rice. It is hard to imagine curry without its fluffy rice bed or a non-rice chicken gumbo or jambalaya. This section includes international dishes which are particularly flavorful. There is a Basque style rice and clam recipe; a spicy Indonesian fried rice; a South American chicken and rice with tomatoes and sausages; an Island flavored dish of papaya filled with chicken and rice; a tender yogurt marinated lamb dish and a curry sauce from India. From closer to home there are orange flavored rice stuffed pork chops, a healthful brown rice meatloaf, stuffed cabbage, and a savory sausage and green pepper casserole.

Rice can be very exciting to eat when combined with flavorful meats, vegetables and spices, and it helps keep your food budget in line.

# BASQUE STYLE RICE AND CLAMS

Serve with a crisp salad for lunch, or fill individual shells or au gratin dishes for a first course.

3 cans (6-1/2 ozs. ea.) chopped clams
1 bottle (8 ozs.) clam juice
1/3 cup olive oil
1/2 cup minced onion
1-1/2 cups uncooked rice
2 large garlic cloves, minced
1/2 cup finely chopped parsley
1 large tomato, peeled, seeded and chopped
pinch of saffron threads (optional)
1 tsp. salt
pepper

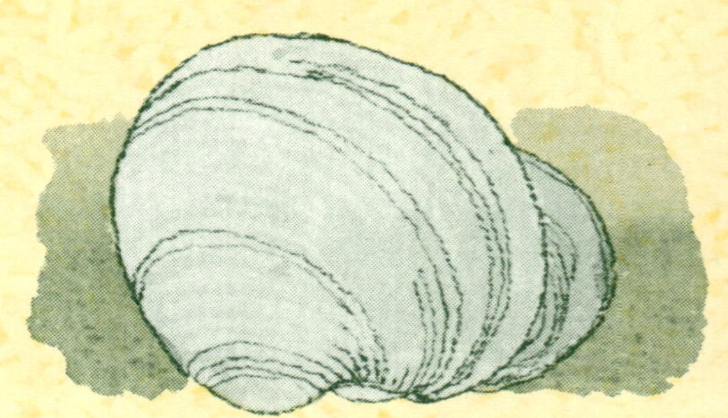

Drain clams and reserve juice. Combine clam juice with bottle of clam juice plus enough water to make 3-1/4 cups total liquid. Heat olive oil in large heavy skillet. Saute onion 5 to 6 minutes until soft. Add rice. Stir until well coated with oil. Add garlic, parsley, chopped tomato, clam juice and water mixture, saffron, salt and pepper. Bring to rapid boil. Cover tightly. Reduce heat to barest simmer. Cook for 20 minutes without lifting lid. Stir in clams. Check rice to see if it is cooked. Add 1/4 cup additional water if rice is not done. Cook covered for a few more minutes. Makes 4 to 6 servings.

**Variation**

To serve for first course—fill individual ovenproof serving dishes with rice and clam mixture. Sprinkle with buttered fresh bread crumbs or Parmesan cheese. Place under broiler for a few minutes to brown lightly. Makes 8 first course servings.

# CHICKEN PAPRIKA

Chicken simmered in a Hungarian-style sauce is served over baked rice.

1 large tomato
1 (3 to 3-1/2 lb.) chicken
flour
salt
3 tbs. butter
2 tbs. brandy
1 small onion, thinly sliced
1/2 cup chopped green pepper
1 small clove garlic, minced
1 tbs. sweet Hungarian paprika
3/4 cup chicken broth
1 tsp. beef extract (Bovril)
1 tsp. lemon juice
1 tsp. salt
3/4 cup sour cream
Baked Rice, page 25

Peel, seed and chop tomato. Set aside. Cut chicken into serving pieces and remove skin. Dust pieces lightly with flour and salt. Melt butter in large skillet. Saute chicken pieces approximately 5 minutes on each side until lightly browned. Turn off heat. Pour in brandy and let warm a minute. Ignite brandy and let burn until flames die. Remove chicken and set aside. Turn heat on. Add onion, pepper and garlic to skillet. Saute over medium heat 3 to 4 minutes until soft. Stir in paprika and cook another minute. Add chicken broth, tomato pieces, beef extract, lemon juice and salt. Bring to boil. Return chicken pieces to skillet. Reduce heat and simmer covered 25 to 30 minutes. In small bowl combine sour cream with 1/2 cup of sauce from skillet. Stir into skillet and heat but do not boil. Serve over baked rice. Makes 4 to 6 servings.

## BAKED RICE

2 tbs. butter
1/2 cup chopped onion
1-1/2 cups cooked rice
3 cups boiling water
1 tsp. salt
1/4 cup chopped parsley
1 cup cooked peas

Melt butter in flameproof casserole. Saute onion 2 to 3 minutes. Add rice and stir until well coated with butter. Cook over low heat about 5 minutes. Add boiling water. Stir in salt. Cover tightly and bake at 350°F. 25 minutes. Add parsley and cooked peas. Fluff rice with a fork. Serve immediately. Makes 4 servings.

# SOUTH AMERICAN CHICKEN AND RICE

This makes a nice party dish or wrap individual servings in foil for a picnic. Serve with an avocado and sliced orange salad.

12 pieces of chicken
juice of 2 limes
1/3 cup olive oil
1 large onion, chopped
2 large green peppers, chopped
2 cloves garlic, minced
1 can (4 ozs.) green chiles
1 can (14 ozs.) Italian style tomatoes
1-1/2 cups uncooked rice
1 bay leaf
1/4 tsp. **each** cumin seed and pepper
1 cup dark beer
1-1/2 cups chicken broth
2 tsp. salt
6 drops Tabasco
4 to 6 mild or hot Italian sausages
1 pkg. (10 ozs.) frozen peas, cooked
1 jar (2 ozs.) chopped pimientos

Marinate chicken in lime juice 10 to 15 minutes. Heat olive oil in large heavy skillet over medium heat. Saute chicken pieces about 30 minutes, turning frequently. Remove chicken from pan. Saute onion, green peppers and garlic until soft but not browned, about 10 minutes. Drain, seed and coarsely chop green chiles. Drain and coarsely chop tomatoes. Add chiles and tomatoes to onion mixture. Stir in rice. Cook over medium heat until rice turns golden, about 4 to 5 minutes. Add bay leaf, cumin, pepper, beer, chicken broth, salt and Tabasco. Stir well. Return chicken to pan. Bring mixture to boil. Cover and simmer over very low heat until rice is tender and liquid has been absorbed. Stir rice mixture frequently. Add more broth if mixture gets too dry before rice is tender. Place sausages in small skillet with 1/2-inch water. Bring to boil. Lower heat and cook covered 10 minutes. Puncture sausages with fork to let out fat. Uncover and cook until nicely browned. Drain on paper towels. Slice in 1/2-inch diagonal slices. Add to rice mixture 10 minutes before rice is done. Place rice and chicken in serving bowl. Garnish with peas and pimientos. Makes 8 servings.

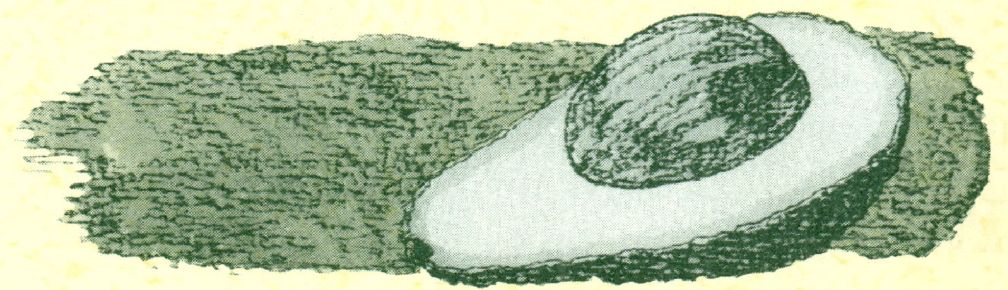

# ISLAND CHICKEN AND PAPAYA

This is an attractive summer luncheon dish for four.

2 large ripe papayas
1 tbs. butter
4 green onions, thinly sliced
1 cup cooked rice
1-1/2 cups cubed cooked chicken
1/2 cup coarsely chopped cashews
1 egg
1/2 tsp. salt
1/4 tsp. white pepper

Cut papayas in half lengthwise. Scoop out seeds and discard. Carefully scoop out papaya fruit, leaving approximately 1/4-inch of fruit and shell. Reserve shells. Coarsely chop papaya fruit and set aside. Melt butter in small saucepan. Saute green onions 2 to 3 minutes until soft. Combine onions, rice, chicken, cashews and chopped papaya. Beat egg with salt and pepper. Combine with chicken mixture. Fill papaya shells, gently pressing the filling into the shells and mounding it as high as possible. Place shells in a baking pan with 1/2-inch water in bottom of pan. Cover pan with foil. Bake in 375°F. oven 20 minutes. Uncover and bake an additional 5 minutes. Serve immediately. Makes 4 servings.

U.S.A.—Harvesting rice by machine in the central valley of California.

# CHICKEN, LAMB OR SEAFOOD CURRY

4 tbs. butter
5 tbs. curry powder
2 large onions, thinly sliced
1 large clove garlic, minced
2 large stalks celery, chopped
1/2 green pepper, chopped
1 large tart green apple, chopped
2 carrots, thinly sliced
2 fresh tomatoes, coarsely chopped
1 tsp. salt
1/4 tsp. thyme
2 bay leaves
1 can (14 ozs.) chicken broth
2 cups water
4 tsp. cornstarch
3 to 4 cups diced cooked chicken or lamb
**or** 1 lb. crab meat or shelled raw shrimp
Perfect Rice, page 58

Melt butter in saucepan. Add curry powder. Cook 2 minutes. Add the next 6 ingredients. Saute 3 to 4 minutes. Add tomatoes, salt, spices, broth and water. Simmer uncovered 2 hours. Strain through a large sieve, pressing as much vegetable pulp through sieve as possible. Return mixture to pan. Dissolve cornstarch in 2 tablespoons water. Add to sauce. Cook, stirring, until sauce thickens. Add chicken, lamb, crab and shrimp. Simmer a few minutes to blend flavors and cook raw shrimp, if used. Serve over rice. Pass coconut, peanuts and chutney. Makes 6 servings.

# CHICKEN GUMBO

3 slices bacon, cut in 1/2-inch pieces
12 chicken thighs, skin removed
1 celery stalk, diced
2 onions, chopped
1 green pepper, chopped
1 can (14 ozs.) Italian style tomatoes
1/2 tsp. thyme
1/4 tsp. white pepper
6 to 8 drops Tabasco
3 cups chicken stock
1/2 cup white wine
1 pkg. (10 ozs.) frozen sliced okra
2 mild or hot Italian sausages, cooked
1/2 cup diced ham (optional)
salt and pepper
Perfect Rice, page 58

Fry bacon in large skillet. Remove and set aside. Dredge chicken in flour if desired. Brown in bacon fat, adding oil if necessary. Remove chicken. Saute onion, green pepper and celery until soft. Chop tomatoes coarsely discarding hard cores and seeds. Add tomatoes with their juice, thyme, pepper, Tabasco, chicken stock and wine to skillet. Bring to boil. Add bacon, chicken, okra, sausage and ham. Simmer covered 30 minutes, stirring occasionally. Remove chicken and pull meat from bones in fairly large pieces. Return to gumbo and cook uncovered 20 minutes. Add salt and pepper to taste. Place rice in bowls and ladle gumbo over rice. Makes 6 servings.

# JAMBALAYA

This is a favorite way to use leftover ham, chicken or shrimp.

4 slices bacon
6 link sausages
1 large onion, coarsely chopped
1 large clove garlic, minced
1 stalk celery, finely diced
1 green pepper, diced
1 cup uncooked rice
2 tbs. tomato paste
1 can (14 ozs.) chicken broth
1 can (14 ozs.) Italian style tomatoes
1/2 tsp. thyme
1/2 tsp. salt
1/8 tsp. ground cloves
1/4 tsp. white pepper
1/4 tsp. chili powder
4 to 6 drops Tabasco
2 cups ham, diced
1/4 cup parsley, minced

Cut bacon into 1-inch pieces. Cut sausages into 1/2-inch slices. Saute together in a large ovenproof skillet until brown. Remove meat. Pour off all but 2 tablespoons fat. Add onion, garlic, celery and green pepper. Saute until onion is soft. Add rice. Stir until well mixed. Add tomato paste, chicken broth, tomatoes with juice, thyme, salt, cloves, pepper, chili powder and Tabasco. Bring to boil. Add ham, sausages, bacon and parsley. Cover tightly. Bake in 350°F. oven for approximately 1 hour. Check from time to time to make sure there is enough liquid. Add 1/4 cup water if necessary. Serve when liquid has been absorbed and rice is tender. Makes 6 servings.

**Variation**

Substitute 2 cups cooked chicken or shrimp. Stir into skillet only about 10 minutes before removing from oven in order not to overcook.

# INDONESIAN FRIED RICE (NASI GORENG)

This spicy dish uses leftover ham, chicken or turkey, and rice.

2 tbs. vegetable oil
1 onion, chopped
1 small clove garlic, minced
1/4 to 1/2 tsp. Spice Islands Hot Pepper Flakes (to taste)
1/2 tsp. **each** salt and sugar
1 tbs. lime juice
2 tbs. **each** brown sugar and soy sauce
1 tbs. water
2-1/2 cups leftover cooked ham, pork, chicken or shrimp
5 cups **cold** cooked rice
Garnishes: Thinly sliced cucumbers, or thinly sliced onions and peppers sauteed in a little butter until soft; or 3 one-egg omelets cut into thin strips

Place oil, onion, garlic, pepper flakes, salt and sugar in blender container. Blend on high speed until mixture is a smooth paste. Scrape down sides once or twice. Set aside. Combine lime juice, brown sugar, soy sauce and water. Place onion paste mixture in a large skillet or wok and saute over medium heat until mixture changes color and turns light brown. Add the lime juice mixture. Stir until blended. Add chopped meat and stir until well coated. Stir in cold rice. Remove from heat for a minute and toss until ingredients are well mixed and rice has an overall brown color. Heat to serving temperature. Serve with garnishes of sliced cucumbers, thinly sliced fried onions and peppers, or 3 one-egg omelets cut into strips. Makes 6 servings.

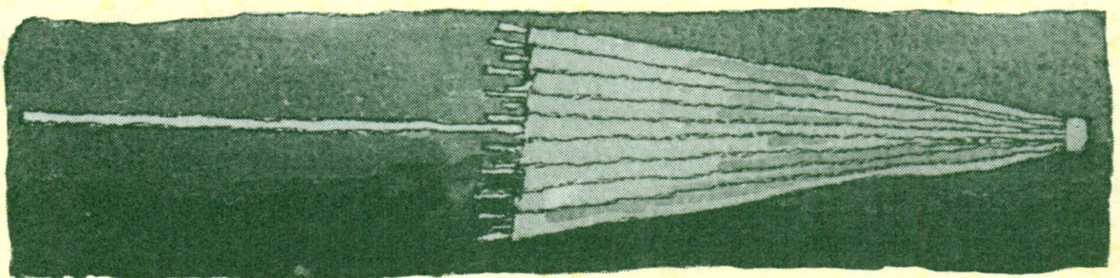

# SAVORY RICE AND SAUSAGE

This quick dish is perfect for luncheon or supper.

1 cup uncooked rice
1 pkg. (2 ozs.) chicken noodle soup mix
3-1/2 cups boiling water
1 lb. bulk pork sausage
1 large onion, chopped
1 green pepper, chopped
2 medium stalks celery, thinly sliced
2 large tomatoes, peeled, seeded and chopped
1/2 tsp. salt
1/4 to 1/2 cup sour cream
3 tbs. grated Parmesan cheese
1 to 2 tbs. butter

Combine rice and noodle soup mix in large saucepan with boiling water. Cover and cook over low heat 20 to 25 minutes until rice is tender. Stir occasionally during cooking. Brown sausage in skillet. Crumble into small pieces with spatula while it cooks. Remove sausage from skillet using a slotted spoon and drain on paper towels. Pour out all but 1 or 2 tablespoons fat. Add onion, pepper and celery to skillet. Saute 4 to 5 minutes until vegetables are soft. In mixing bowl combine cooked rice, sausage, vegetables, tomatoes and salt. Mix in enough sour cream to moisten. Place in greased casserole. Sprinkle with Parmesan cheese and dot with butter. Bake in 375°F. oven 15 to 20 minutes until casserole is hot and top is slightly browned. Makes 6 to 8 servings.

**Variations**

Add 1/2 cup sliced sauteed fresh mushrooms to casserole.

Use as a stuffing for green peppers or fresh tomatoes. (Parboil green peppers 5 minutes.) Fill with sausage mixture and bake uncovered for 20 minutes at 375°F.

If you have any of the casserole leftover, stir in 1 tablespoon soy sauce, and combine with 2 lightly scrambled eggs for a quick fried rice dish for breakfast or lunch.

U.S.A.—The old way of selling rice, from barrel to paper bag.

# ORANGE RICE STUFFED PORK CHOPS

1 tbs. butter
5 to 6 green onions, thinly sliced
1 cup cooked rice
1 tsp. grated orange rind
1/2 cup fresh orange juice
2 tbs. sugar
1/2 tsp. thyme
1 tsp. salt
1/4 cup raisins
4 double pork chops
with pockets for stuffing
2 tbs. oil

Melt butter in small skillet. Saute green onions 2 to 3 minutes until soft. Combine rice, orange rind, **1/4** cup orange juice, sugar, thyme, salt, raisins and cooked onions. Stuff pork chops with rice mixture. Use toothpicks to hold stuffing in pockets. Heat oil in large skillet. Quickly brown chops on both sides. Place browned chops in oiled baking dish. Pour remaining orange juice around chops. Cover tightly. Bake at 325°F. for 30 to 45 minutes, depending on size of chops. Uncover and bake another 30 to 45 minutes. Makes 4 servings.

Note: Pork chops can be stuffed ahead and refrigerated.

# DAD'S SPANISH RICE

This recipe is a family favorite. It is better made a day ahead and reheated.

2 cups water
3/4 cup uncooked rice
1 tbs. vegetable oil
2 lbs. ground beef
1 onion, chopped
2 stalks celery, diced
2 cans (10 ozs. ea.) tomato soup
1/2 cup catsup
1 tbs. Worcestershire sauce
1 tbs. vinegar
2 tbs. sugar
1 tbs. chili powder
1/4 tsp. salt

Bring water to boil in medium saucepan. Add rice. Cover and cook over low heat

12 minutes then drain off excess water. While rice is cooking heat oil in large skillet. Saute onion and celery until soft but not brown. Remove from skillet and set aside. Saute ground beef in skillet crumbling into small pieces as it cooks. Pour off fat. Add onion and celery, tomato soup, catsup, Worcestershire, vinegar, sugar, chili powder, salt and drained rice to skillet. Simmer 10 to 15 minutes to blend flavors. Stir as little as possible. Makes 6 to 8 servings.

# STUFFED CABBAGE LEAVES

Make ahead of time and reheat. They also freeze well.

1/2 cup uncooked long grain rice
1 tbs. vegetable oil
1 medium onion, finely chopped
1 clove garlic, minced
3/4 lb. lean ground beef
3/4 lb. lean ground pork
1/2 tsp. salt
1/4 tsp. white pepper
dash nutmeg

1 large head cabbage
2 cups tomato or V-8 juice
1 tbs. meat extract (Bovril)
2 tbs. tomato paste
6 to 8 drops Tabasco
1/2 tsp. sweet basil
2 tbs. flour
1/4 cup sour cream

Parboil rice in a large pot of boiling salted water for 5 minutes. Drain well in sieve. Set aside. Heat oil in skillet. Saute onion until transparent. Combine rice, onion, garlic, beef, pork, salt, pepper and nutmeg. Mix well. Cut base from cabbage. Remove core. Immerse in boiling water to soften leaves. Let stand for a few minutes. Peel off leaves as they soften and water cools enough to handle the cabbage. Remove the large ribs from the stem end of leaves. Place about 2 tablespoons filling on each leaf. Fold sides of leaf over filling. Roll up into a neat package. Continue until all filling is used. Put two leaves together if you run out of large leaves. Chop the remaining small leaves and trimmings and put into a lightly oiled baking dish. Place cabbage rolls on top of chopped cabbage seam side down. Arrange them very closely together so they will fit in a single layer. Combine tomato juice, meat extract, tomato paste, Tabasco and sweet basil. Pour over cabbage rolls. Cover dish tightly with lid or aluminum foil. Bake in a 325°F. oven for 2 hours. Combine flour and sour cream and leave at room temperature until needed. When cabbage rolls are done, carefully remove them to a heated platter and keep warm. Strain pan juices and discard shredded cabbage. Return strained juice to pan and heat almost to boiling. Add sour cream and stir until thickened. Pour sauce over cabbage rolls and serve. Makes approximately 2 dozen rolls.

# SWISS STEAK WITH RICE

2 lbs. round steak, approx. 1 in. thick
flour, salt, and pepper for dredging
3 tbs. vegetable oil
1 large onion, thinly sliced
2 medium carrots, diced
2 small fresh green chile peppers
**or** 1 large green pepper, diced
1 clove garlic, minced
1 can (14 ozs.) Italian style tomatoes with juice
1 can (14 ozs.) Swanson's beef broth
1/2 cup dry red wine
1/2 tsp. oregano
2 tbs. soy sauce
1 cup uncooked rice

Trim round steak and cut into 2-inch pieces. Score steak approximately 1/4-inch deep on both sides. Dredge in flour, salt, and pepper. Heat oil in large heavy skillet.

Brown meat on both sides. Remove meat from pan and set aside. Saute onions, carrots, chile peppers and garlic in remaining oil until onion is soft. Add tomatoes, beef broth, red wine, oregano and soy sauce. Bring to boil. Return steak to pan. Cover and simmer over low heat until meat is tender, approximately 2 hours. Stir in rice. Cover and continue cooking 20 to 25 minutes until rice is tender. Makes 4 to 5 servings.

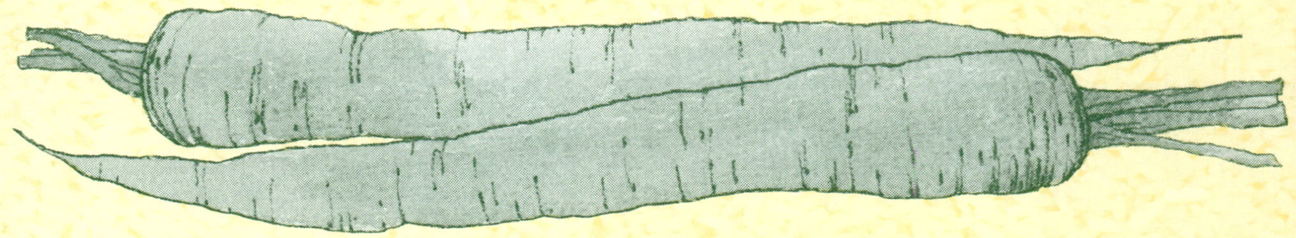

# CHILI RICE

2 lbs. round steak, approx. 1/2 in. thick
1/4 cup vegetable oil
1-1/2 cups coarsely chopped onion
2 cloves garlic, minced
2 tbs. chili powder
1/2 tsp. oregano
1/4 tsp. cinnamon
1 tsp. ground cumin seed
1/2 tsp. Spice Islands crushed red pepper
1 can (14 ozs.) Swanson's beef broth
1 can (14 ozs.) Italian style tomatoes
2 tbs. tomato paste
1-1/2 tsp. salt
1 tbs. brown sugar
freshly ground black pepper
1 cup cooked rice

Cut round steak into 1/2-inch cubes. Heat vegetable oil in large heavy skillet or dutch oven with lid. Dry steak cubes on paper towels. Saute in hot oil until meat changes color. Add onion. Cook, stirring, 2 to 3 minutes. Add garlic, chili powder, oregano, cinnamon, cumin and red pepper. Mix well. Stir in beef broth, tomatoes with their juice, tomato paste, salt, brown sugar and pepper. Break up tomatoes with spatula. Mix well. Simmer covered 1 hour over very low heat. Uncover and cook 30 minutes, stirring more frequently as sauce thickens. Stir in rice. Simmer until heated, about 10 minutes. Makes 6 servings.

CHINA—Transplanting young shoots from seed beds to fields that have been flooded.

# BROWN RICE MEATLOAF

2 tbs. butter
1 medium onion, chopped
8 to 10 fresh mushrooms, coarsely chopped
1 lb. ground meat (half pork and half beef, or any combination)
2 eggs
1 cup cooked brown rice
2 tsp. **each** Worcestershire sauce and Dijon mustard
2 tbs. tomato paste
1 tsp. salt
pepper
2 strips bacon

Melt butter in skillet. Saute onions and mushrooms until mushrooms are cooked. Combine meat, eggs, rice, onions, mushrooms, Worcestershire, mustard, tomato paste, salt and pepper. Press into a loaf pan, leaving an inch at ends of pan to collect fat. Top with bacon slices. Bake in a 375°F. oven 1 hour and 10 minutes. Using a baster or spoon remove excess fat once or twice during baking. Makes 4 servings.

# BAKED LAMB AND RICE CASSEROLE

2 lbs. lean, boneless lamb
2 tbs. oil
2 tbs. butter
1 medium onion, diced
1 small green pepper, diced
1-1/2 cups uncooked long grain rice
1 tsp. salt
1/4 tsp. basil
1/2 tsp. oregano
1 can (8 ozs.) tomato sauce
2 cans (11 ozs.) beef broth
1/3 cup dry sherry

Cut lamb into 1 to 1-1/2-inch cubes. Heat oil in large heavy skillet. Brown lamb cubes. Remove meat and pour off all fat. Add butter, onions and green pepper. Cook slowly until onion and peppers are soft but not brown. Add rice, salt, basil and oregano. Cook 3 to 4 minutes until rice is opaque. Add lamb, tomato sauce, beef broth and sherry. Bring to boil and simmer 4 to 5 minutes. Pour into casserole with tightly fitting lid. Bake at 350°F. 45 minutes to 1 hour, or until liquid is absorbed and rice is tender. Makes 4 to 6 servings.

# LAMB IN NUT YOGURT SAUCE

2 lbs. boneless leg of lamb
1/4 cup clarified butter*
1-1/2 cups yellow onions, chopped
2 cloves garlic, minced
1/2 tsp. tumeric
1/4 tsp. powdered cardamom
1/4 tsp. cinnamon
1/2 tsp. black pepper
1 tsp. salt
1 cup plain yogurt
2 cups water
1/2 cup ground blanched almonds
1/3 cup heavy cream
1/3 cup fresh cilantro leaves, very finely chopped
Perfect Rice, page 58

Trim fat from lamb and cut into 1-inch cubes. Heat clarified butter in heavy saucepan. Add onion and saute until golden. Add garlic, tumeric, cardamom, cinnamon and black pepper. Stir for a minute. Add lamb cubes. Toss gently to coat lamb with spice-onion mixture. Add salt, yogurt and water. Cover pot. Simmer gently over low heat for 45 minutes. Remove cover and increase heat. Continue cooking until meat is very tender and most of liquid is absorbed. (The meat mixture can be cooled and refrigerated for a day or two at this point, or frozen.) Add ground almonds. Simmer for 10 minutes. Add cream and cilantro at the last minute before serving and heat just to serving temperature. Serve with Perfect Rice. Makes 4 to 5 servings.

*To clarify, melt butter in small saucepan over low heat. When butter becomes foamy skim off foam with a tablespoon. Carefully pour off clear liquid and leave milky solids in bottom of pan. Use clear butter liquid and discard milk solids.

# SPINACH AND RICE BAKE

This is a good luncheon or picnic dish served at room temperature.

1 pkg. (10 ozs.) frozen chopped spinach
1 tbs. butter
6 to 7 green onions, thinly sliced
1 clove garlic, minced
5 eggs
1 cup **each** milk and cooked rice
1/2 cup diced Swiss or cheddar cheese
1/4 cup chopped parsley
1 tsp. dried dill weed
1/4 tsp. marjoram
pinch of nutmeg and white pepper
Parmesan cheese for topping

Cook spinach according to package directions. Drain spinach and squeeze very dry. Melt butter in small skillet. Saute onions and garlic 2 to 3 minutes until onion

softens. Lightly beat eggs with milk. Combine spinach, onions, rice, cheese, parsley, dill weed, marjoram, nutmeg and white pepper. Add eggs and milk. Mix well. Pour into greased 1-1/2 quart casserole. Sprinkle with Parmesan cheese. Bake in 350°F. oven 30 to 35 minutes until casserole is puffed and lightly browned. Cut in slices to serve. Makes 4 to 6 servings.

**Variation** — 2 cups cooked chopped broccoli can be substituted for spinach.

# EGGPLANT RICE CASSEROLE

4 to 6 tbs. olive oil
1 large eggplant, peeled
1 medium onion, chopped
1/2 green pepper, chopped
1 clove garlic, minced
1/2 lb. ground beef
1/4 cup red wine
2 cans (8 ozs. ea.) tomato sauce
1/2 tsp. oregano
1/4 tsp. cumin seed
1/2 tsp. salt
pepper
1-1/2 cups cooked rice
Parmesan cheese

Cut eggplant into 1/4-inch slices. Heat 3 tablespoons olive oil in large skillet. Saute eggplant slices 2 to 3 minutes on each side until tender. Remove and drain on paper towels. Add more oil as necessary. Saute onion, green pepper and garlic in same skillet until onions and peppers are soft. Remove. Brown ground beef. Break into small pieces with spatula as it cooks. Pour off fat. Return onions and peppers to skillet. Stir in wine and 1-1/2 cans tomato sauce. Add oregano, cumin seed, salt and pepper. Simmer over low heat uncovered for 20 minutes to blend flavors. Stir in rice. Arrange one layer of eggplant slices in bottom of greased casserole. Spoon half of meat mixture over eggplant. Add another layer of eggplant and top with the rest of meat mixture. Pour remaining tomato sauce over meat mixture. Sprinkle with Parmesan cheese. Bake covered in 350°F. oven 20 to 25 minutes. Makes 4 servings.

CHINA—A large cooperative work force is needed to harvest the rice crops of the world's most populous country

# SIDE DISHES

For variety choose a rice dish instead of potatoes to complete your dinner menu. Serve Perfect Rice, page 58, with its lovely separate grains when you have a flavorful meat or vegetable sauce. Cook rice in tomato or orange juice, or chicken broth to give it added flavor or stir in fresh herbs or chopped nuts for a crunchy texture. Make a Tomato Rice Souffle for a colorful and tasty accompaniment to lamb or pork chops. Or serve a pretty mushroom risotto in a ring mold with a center of fresh cooked green vegetables for a buffet table. Try an orange rice pilaf with white raisins and almonds for an elegant accompaniment to chicken or pork. Rice also makes an excellent stuffing for tomatoes, eggplant, or green peppers.

Wild rice, while not really in the rice family, makes a delicious side dish for poultry or game.

# PERFECT RICE

Here is a recipe for perfectly cooked, each grain separate, fluffy rice. If desired, the amount of uncooked rice can be decreased to 2 cups without affecting the recipe.

2-1/2 cups uncooked long grain rice
3 tbs. salt
3 tbs. butter

Heat 4 to 6 quarts of water to boiling in a large kettle. Add salt and rice. Boil vigorously, uncovered, for 15 minutes. Pour rice into strainer to drain. Rinse with cold water. Melt butter in a large heavy saucepan. Stir in well drained rice. Wrap lid of saucepan with a dish towel so that towel is between lid and saucepan. Place over very low heat and steam 25 minutes without lifting lid. Remove from heat. Rice will wait until you are ready to serve it for at least an hour. Toss lightly with a fork just before serving. Makes 6 servings.

Note: If using Basmati rice, decrease boiling time to 10 minutes.

# ORANGE RICE PILAF

Good accompaniment for ham, turkey or roast pork.

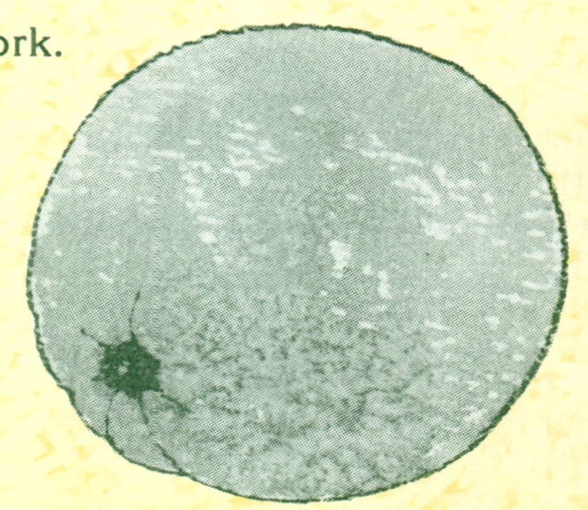

4 tbs. butter
1 medium onion, finely chopped
1 cup uncooked rice
grated rind of 1 orange
juice of two oranges **plus** enough
chicken broth to make 2-1/4 cups liquid
1/2 tsp. salt
slivered almonds and white raisins

Melt butter in large saucepan. Saute onion until soft but not brown. Add rice to pan. Stir until rice is well coated with butter and turns a milky or translucent color (approximately 5 minutes). Add orange rind, orange juice plus chicken broth and salt. Bring to boil. Cover and cook over very low heat approximately 20 to 25 minutes until rice is tender and liquid is absorbed. Stir in slivered almonds and raisins. Makes 6 side dish servings.

# ARMENIAN RICE PILAF

This is a perfect dish to serve with shish kebob.

3 cans (14 ozs. ea.) chicken broth
1 cube butter
1/2 cup crushed fine egg noodles
2 cups uncooked long grain rice

Bring chicken broth to boil in saucepan. Melt 4 tablespoons butter in a 3-quart flameproof casserole with tightly fitting lid. Add crushed egg noodles to melted butter and stir until golden brown. Add boiling broth and rice and stir gently. Boil 5 minutes. Cover casserole and place in a 350°F. oven 20 to 25 minutes, or until all liquid is absorbed. Stir gently and dot with remaining butter. Return to oven and bake uncovered for 5 minutes. Serve immediately. Makes 4 to 6 servings.

# BAKED RICE AND LENTILS

3 tbs. butter
1 small onion, chopped
1/2 tsp. cumin
1/2 cup lentils
1 cup uncooked long grain rice
1 can (14 ozs.) chicken broth
3/4 cup water
1 tsp. salt

Melt butter in flameproof casserole. Saute onion until soft, but not browned. Stir in cumin and cook 2 to 3 minutes longer. Add lentils, rice, chicken stock, water and salt. Bring mixture to boil. Cover and place in 375°F. oven. Bake 20 to 25 minutes until liquid is absorbed and rice is tender. Makes 4 servings.

Note: If you prefer less crunchy lentils, cover lentils with boiling water and let stand for 15 minutes before adding to onion.

# CARIBBEAN RICE

Serve with spareribs or chicken. Coconut milk definitely makes a difference.

2 tbs. vegetable oil
1 medium onion, finely chopped
2 small fresh chili peppers, seeded and finely chopped
1 cup uncooked rice
2 cups liquid—coconut milk* plus juice from red kidney beans
1 can (15-1/4 ozs.) red kidney beans
1/4 tsp. thyme
1 tsp. salt
pepper

Heat oil in small skillet. Saute onion and peppers in oil until soft but not brown. Combine onions and peppers in large saucepan with rice, coconut milk and bean juice (plus water if necessary to make 2 cups), thyme, salt and pepper. Bring to boil. Cover and simmer over very low heat 20 to 25 minutes until rice is cooked. Stir in kidney beans and cook another 5 minutes. Makes 4 to 6 servings.

***Prepared from fresh coconut:** If your fresh coconut has a husk on it, either drop it on concrete or some other hard surface, or hit it with a sledge hammer. The husk should split so the fiber-covered nut can be taken out. Shake the nut and if it sloshes, it is fresh. Pierce one of the three black holes at the top to drain out liquid and discard. Tap the nut with a hammer to break it open. Trim the coconut meat from the brown rind. Cut into fairly small pieces and place in blender container with 1 cup water. Blend on high speed until smooth. Strain through a sieve pressing out as much liquid as possible. Reserve liquid. Put coconut pulp back into blender container with another cup of water. Blend. Strain again and discard pulp. Combine bean juice and coconut milk to make 2 cups liquid.

**Prepared from dried unsweetened coconut meal** (available in health food stores) — Pour 1 cup boiling water over 1/2 cup coconut meal. Let stand 5 minutes. Strain into a 2-cup measure, pressing out as much liquid as possible. Discard coconut meal. Drain kidney bean juice into measure with coconut milk. Add water to make 2 cups. Use as directed.

# MUSHROOM RISOTTO

Fill this elegant ring mold with sauteed cherry tomatoes or a cooked green vegetable.

3-1/2 to 4 cups chicken broth
1/4 cup butter
1 clove garlic, minced
1/2 lb. fresh mushrooms, thinly sliced
1/2 cup chopped parsley
1/2 tsp. salt
white pepper
1/4 cup butter
1 small onion, thinly sliced
1-1/2 cups uncooked short grain rice
1/3 cup dry white wine or dry vermouth
1/2 cup grated Parmesan cheese

Heat chicken broth. Melt butter in a medium sized skillet. Add garlic and

mushrooms. Saute over high heat 3 to 4 minutes, stirring frequently. Add parsley and cook another minute. Remove from heat and set aside. Melt 1/4 cup butter in a 2-quart saucepan. Add onion slices. Cook until onion is soft but not brown. Add rice and cook over medium heat until rice is opaque, approximately 5 to 6 minutes. Add hot chicken broth 1/4 cup at a time, stirring constantly. As rice absorbs the liquid, add more. Pour in wine. Stir until it is absorbed. When rice is creamy and tender, add half of the sauteed mushrooms. Mix well. Remove from heat and stir in Parmesan cheese. Place remaining mushrooms in the bottom of a buttered ring mold. Spoon cooked rice into mold and pack it gently. Invert and unmold on a warm platter. Fill center with cherry tomatoes that have been sauteed in butter for approximately 2 minutes, or a cooked green vegetable. Serve immediately. Makes 4 to 6 servings.

JAPAN—Two women transplant rice seedlings near their small farming village.

# CHEDDAR AND BROWN RICE

This nutritious dish is a good accompaniment for steaks or chicken.

2 tbs. butter
1 medium onion, chopped
3 cups cooked brown rice
3 to 4 tbs. fresh cilantro, chopped
1 can (4 ozs.) green chiles, drained, seeded and chopped
1 cup grated cheddar cheese
1/4 tsp. cumin
1/2 tsp. salt
1-1/4 cups sour cream

Melt butter in small skillet. Saute onion until soft. Combine onions, rice, cilantro, green chiles, cheddar cheese, cumin, salt and sour cream. Mix well. Place in greased casserole and bake in 350°F. oven 20 to 25 minutes until hot. Makes 4 servings.

# QUICK FRIED RICE

3 tbs. vegetable oil
1 tsp. sesame oil
1 cup finely chopped ham, chicken, sausage or shrimp
4 green onions, thinly sliced
2 tbs. soy sauce
1/4 tsp. white pepper
3 eggs
3 cups cold cooked rice

Heat both oils in medium skillet. Saute chopped meat and onions together until onion is softened, about 3 to 4 minutes. Combine soy sauce and white pepper with eggs. Mix lightly. Add egg mixture to meat. Stir quickly to scramble eggs, breaking them into small pieces with spatula. Add rice. Stir, lifting meat egg mixture through rice until rice is hot. Makes 4 side dish servings or 2 luncheon portions.

## MEXICAN STYLE FRIED RICE

This is a good side dish with barbecued meats or enchiladas.

1 cup uncooked long grain rice
3 tbs. peanut oil
1/4 cup minced onion
1 small clove garlic, minced
1/2 cup fresh tomatoes, peeled, seeded and chopped
1 tbs. tomato paste
1 cup chicken broth
1/2 tsp. salt

Boil rice in a large quantity of rapidly boiling salted water for 8 minutes. Drain rice in colander. Heat oil in an ovenproof-flameproof casserole. Add onion, garlic, and rice. Stir over medium heat until rice is golden, about 5 minutes. Add tomato pieces and cook another minute. Stir in tomato paste and chicken broth. Bring to boil and cook without stirring until large holes appear in rice. Cover tightly with lid or aluminum foil. Place in a 300°F. oven. Bake for 30 minutes without lifting cover. Fluff with a fork and serve. Makes 4 servings.

# TOMATOES STUFFED WITH RICE

This makes a colorful side dish to serve with barbecued lamb or steaks.

4 large tomatoes
3 tbs. butter
6 green onions, thinly sliced
1 tsp. sweet basil
1/2 tsp. marjoram
1/2 tsp. salt
1/4 tsp..white pepper
1-1/2 cups cooked rice
Parmesan cheese
butter

Cut a half-inch slice off top of tomatoes. Carefully cut around the center of each tomato with a small knife, leaving a one-half inch shell. Remove centers with small sharp spoon and coarsely chop. Rinse out tomatoes to remove seeds. Sprinkle the inside of each tomato shell with a little salt. Turn shells upside down on a plate to drain

for approximately 20 minutes. Heat butter in a small skillet. Saute green onions 2 to 3 minutes until soft. Add basil, marjoram, salt, pepper, rice and chopped tomato centers to skillet. Mix well. Stuff tomato shells with rice mixture. Sprinkle with Parmesan and dot with butter. Place tomatoes in small baking dish with one-half inch water in bottom of dish. Bake in a 375°F. oven 15 minutes if tomatoes are very ripe, and 20 minutes if they are very firm. Serve immediately. Makes 4 servings.

**Variation** — Parboil green pepper shells for 5 minutes. Stuff with rice mixture substituting 1/2 cup sliced sauteed fresh mushrooms for the tomato pieces. Bake uncovered for 20 minutes at 375°F.

# TOMATO RICE SOUFFLE

1/4 cup butter
4 to 5 green onions, thinly sliced
1/4 cup flour
1-1/2 cups milk
1/3 cup Parmesan cheese
5 eggs, separated
1 cup cooked rice
4 medium tomatoes
1/2 tsp. sweet basil
1/2 tsp. thyme
1 tsp. salt
white pepper

Melt butter in saucepan. Saute onions until soft. Add flour and cook 2 minutes. Gradually add milk. Cook until sauce thickens. Stir in Parmesan cheese. Lightly beat egg yolks. Stir a little of the hot sauce into egg yolks and carefully add warmed yolks to rest of sauce. Stir in cooked rice. Peel, seed and chop tomatoes. Squeeze as much juice as possible out of the tomatoes and add to sauce along with basil, thyme, salt and pepper. Beat egg whites until very stiff. Fold egg whites into tomato rice mixture with a rubber spatula. Do not overmix. Pour into buttered 1-1/2-quart souffle dish. Bake in 350°F. oven 30 to 35 minutes, or until souffle is puffed and lightly browned. Serve immediately. Makes 6 servings.

# WALNUT WILD RICE

1/3 cup wild rice
3-1/2 cups boiling water
2/3 cup uncooked long grain rice
1 tsp. salt
2 tbs. butter
4 to 5 green onions, thinly sliced
1 small clove garlic, minced
1/2 cup coarsely chopped walnuts

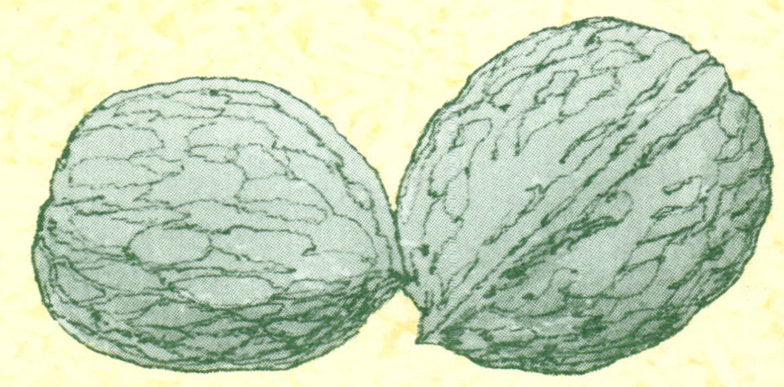

Place wild rice in a small bowl. Cover with 1 cup boiling water. Let stand 5 minutes. Drain. Combine wild rice, long grain rice and salt in medium saucepan. Add 2-1/2 cups boiling water. Place over low heat, cover and simmer 25 to 30 minutes until liquid is absorbed. Melt butter in small skillet. Saute green onions and garlic 4 to 5 minutes until soft. When rice is tender stir in green onion mixture and chopped walnuts. Serve immediately. Makes 4 servings.

# WILD RICE SOUFFLE

This is an elegant accompaniment for roast duck or pork.

1/4 cup wild rice
1-1/2 cups beef or chicken broth
3 tbs. butter
3 tbs. flour
1/2 cup milk or chicken broth
1/4 lb. fresh mushrooms, thinly sliced
5 green onions, thinly sliced
2 tbs. butter
4 egg yolks
1/4 tsp. white pepper
1/2 tsp. salt
1/2 tsp. tarragon
5 egg whites

Cook wild rice in broth for 1 hour, or until tender. Not all of the liquid will be absorbed by the rice but do not drain. Set aside. Melt butter in saucepan. Add flour and cook 2 minutes. Gradually add milk. Stir in wild rice and liquid. Cook until sauce thickens. Saute mushrooms and green onions in butter for 3 to 4 minutes until mushrooms are cooked. Add egg yolks to rice mixture along with pepper, salt and tarragon. Stir in mushrooms and green onions. Beat egg whites until stiff. Gently beat a small amount of egg whites into rice mixture to lighten. Fold in remaining egg whites. Pour into a well buttered 2-quart souffle dish. Bake at 375°F. for 30 to 35 minutes until top is puffed and lightly browned. Serve immediately. Makes 6 servings.

Note: Wild rice can be cooked a day or two ahead of time and refrigerated until you are ready to use it.

BURMA—A young woman winnowing rice in the breeze.

# DESSERTS

Rice may be used in classic as well as simple desserts. It combines beautifully with dessert ingredients of cream, sugar, vanilla and fresh fruit. Round or medium grain rice should be used for most creamy rice desserts because it cooks more completely and has a soft texture.

For an elegant dessert consider the classic French molded rice dessert, Riz a l' Imperatrice, which can be garnished with fresh or candied fruits or a fruit sauce. Or try a Sweet Orange Rice Souffle for an impressive finish to a special dinner.

Brown rice also works well in desserts and it gives a nutty flavor and crunchy texture to our apple crisp.

Included also are a delicious creamy Coconut Rice Custard and a baked Rice Flan, both of which are beautiful with fresh fruit in season, and an Old Fashioned Rice Pudding just like Grandma used to make.

# RICE CHEESECAKE

Make this dessert in a ring mold and fill center with sweetened fresh fruit.

1-1/2 cups cooked rice
1/2 cup milk
3 eggs, separated
1/3 cup sugar
1/2 tsp. vanilla
1/4 cup lemon juice
2 tbs. apricot or orange liqueur
1 tbs. unflavored gelatin
1 cup creamed cottage cheese
1 cup sour cream
1/3 cup sugar
1/2 cup heavy cream

Cook rice in milk over very low heat for 20 minutes, stirring frequently. Beat egg yolks with sugar. Add some of hot rice to egg yolks and carefully add warm yolks to rest of hot rice. Cook over low heat 2 to 3 minutes. Combine vanilla, lemon juice and apricot liqueur. Soften gelatin in mixture and add to hot rice custard. Stir until gelatin is dissolved. Place cottage cheese, sour cream and rice mixture in blender container. Blend until smooth and creamy. Cool. When barely warm beat egg whites with 1/3 cup sugar until stiff. Whip cream until stiff. Fold egg whites and cream into rice mixture. Pour into large oiled ring mold, or individual serving dishes. Chill for several hours until firm. Unmold and serve with sweetened fresh fruit. Makes 6 to 8 servings.

# RICE FLAN

1/4 cup uncooked medium
round grain or Calrose rice
1-1/2 cups milk
1/2 cup sugar
3 eggs
1/3 cup sugar
2 cups milk
1/2 tsp. vanilla
2 tbs. orange liqueur or orange juice

Cook rice with milk over very low heat, covered, for about 40 minutes. Stir occasionally. Rice should be quite soft. Let cool for a few minutes. Melt 1/2 cup sugar in small skillet over medium heat until sugar carmelizes and turns a light brown. Remove from heat immediately and pour into a 6 cup ring mold. Beat eggs with 1/3 cup sugar. Stir in milk, vanilla and orange liqueur. Add cooled rice. Spoon custard into ring mold, distributing rice as evenly as possible. Set mold in pan of boiling water so water comes halfway up sides of mold. Bake in a 375°F. oven 30 to 45 minutes, until knife blade inserted near center comes out clean. Let cool slightly and refrigerate. Serve cold. Unmold by running knife blade around edge of flan. Place serving dish on top of mold and quickly invert. The carmel makes a little sauce for the flan. Fill center of mold with fresh fruit, or serve plain. Makes 6 servings.

# COCONUT RICE CUSTARD

This creamy dessert is delicious as is, or it can be topped with fresh strawberries, peaches or raspberries.

2 cups milk
3 eggs
1/2 cup sugar
pinch of salt
3/4 cup cooked rice
1/2 cup sweetened, flaked coconut
2 tsp. vanilla

Scald milk in top of double boiler. Beat eggs, sugar and salt together. Stir a little of the warm milk into eggs. Carefully add egg mixture to remaining milk. Continue to cook over low heat. Stir constantly until mixture thickens slightly and coats back of spoon. Remove from heat. Stir in cooked rice, coconut and vanilla. When custard cools slightly, press plastic wrap directly onto custard to keep skin from forming. Chill well before serving. Makes 6 servings.

# OLD FASHIONED RICE PUDDING

3 to 4 cups water
1 cup short grain rice
4 cups milk
1 cinnamon stick
2/3 cup sugar
1/2 cup raisins
1 tsp. vanilla
1/8 tsp. lemon extract

Bring water to boil and add rice. Parboil for 5 minutes. Drain rice in sieve. Combine milk, cinnamon stick, sugar and raisins in saucepan. Bring to boil. Add drained rice. Reduce heat and simmer partially covered 30 to 35 minutes, stirring occasionally. When mixture is still creamy and rice is tender, remove from heat. Stir in vanilla and lemon extract. Let cool to room temperature then refrigerate until well chilled. Discard cinnamon stick before serving. Makes 6 to 8 servings.

BURMA—In this country where two-thirds of the land is planted in rice, a woman takes her crop to market by boat.

# RIZ A L'IMPERATRICE

This is a classic elegant rice dessert. Garnish it with candied fruits, or serve it with fresh strawberries or an orange sauce.

1/3 cup uncooked medium or round grain rice
2 cups milk
2 tbs. butter
1 env. unflavored gelatin
2 tbs. apricot liqueur
2 tbs. Triple Sec or orange juice
1 cup milk
2 eggs

1/3 cup sugar
1/4 tsp. salt
1/2 tsp. vanilla
1/8 cup candied lemon peel
1/8 cup candied orange peel
1 cup heavy cream
1/4 cup sugar

Oil a 6 cup mold and set aside. Cook rice and milk together in a covered saucepan 40 minutes or until rice is very tender. Stir occasionally to prevent sticking. Milk will not be completely absorbed. Stir in butter. Set aside. Soften gelatin in apricot and Triple Sec liqueurs. Heat milk in top of double boiler. Beat together eggs, 1/3 cup sugar and salt. Gradually add to hot milk. Cook over simmering water, stirring constantly until mixture thickens slightly and coats the back of a spoon. Remove from heat. Add vanilla and softened gelatin. Stir until gelatin is dissolved. Let cool slightly. Dice candied lemon and orange peel very finely. Stir diced fruit and cooked rice into custard. Place pan with custard rice mixture in a large bowl filled with ice cubes and water. Stir until custard is completely cool and starts to set. Whip cream with 1/4 cup sugar until very stiff. Fold into the partially thickened custard. Pour mixture into mold. Chill at least 4 hours until very firm. To unmold, run knife blade around edge of mold. Set mold in pan of warm water for 10 seconds. Place chilled serving plate on top of mold and quickly invert. Remove mold and garnish dessert with a candied fruit design, or surround with fresh sliced strawberries or peaches moistened with a tablespoon of orange or apricot liqueur. Makes 8 servings.

Note: 1/2 cup of mixed candied fruits may be substituted for orange and lemon peel.

# SWEET ORANGE RICE SOUFFLE

1/2 cup Minute rice
1-2/3 cups milk
1/4 cup butter
1/4 cup flour
grated rind from 1 orange
juice from 2 oranges **plus** enough water to make 2/3 cup liquid
5 eggs, separated
5 tbs. Triple Sec
salt
1/4 cup sugar
1 cup heavy cream
2 tbs. powdered sugar

Cook Minute rice with 1 cup milk in top of double boiler for 45 minutes until very soft. Set aside. This can be done ahead of time and refrigerated. Melt butter in medium saucepan. Add flour and cook 2 minutes. Stir in orange rind, orange juice and 2/3 cup milk. Cook until mixture thickens. Stir a little of hot sauce into lightly beaten egg yolks. Carefully add warmed egg yolks to hot sauce. Add rice, 3 tablespoons Triple Sec and salt. Beat egg whites and 1/4 cup sugar until stiff. Gently fold beaten egg whites into sauce. Pour into a generously buttered 2-quart souffle dish. Bake in 375°F. oven 30 to 35 minutes until puffed and lightly browned. Whip cream with powdered sugar and remaining 2 tablespoons Triple Sec. Serve souffle immediately with a dollop of flavored whipped cream. Makes 4 servings.

# BROWN RICE APPLE CRISP

A different version of an old favorite.

3 large cooking apples, peeled and sliced
2 cups cooked brown rice
1/2 tsp. cinnamon
nutmeg
1 tbs. lemon juice
1 cup brown sugar
1/3 cup soft butter
1/2 cup flour

Place half of the apple slices in a buttered 8 x 8-inch baking dish. Top with rice and 1/4 teaspoon cinnamon. Add remaining apples. Sprinkle with nutmeg and lemon juice. Blend together brown sugar, butter, flour and remaining cinnamon until mixture is like coarse meal. Spread over apples. Press down firmly. Bake in 350°F. oven 40 to 45 minutes. Makes 4 to 6 servings.

# INDEX

With many thanks to our special friend,
Gayle Morais

# Pasta

by
**Coleen and Bob Simmons**

Illustrated by
**Craig Torlucci**

A Nitty Gritty Book*
Published by
Nitty Gritty Productions
P.O. Box 5457
Concord, California 94524

*Nitty Girtty Books — Trademark
Owned by Nitty Gritty Productions
Concord, California

ISBN 0-911954-49-X
Library of Congress Catalog Card Number:
78-71487

ISBN 0-911954-49-X

# TABLE OF CONTENTS

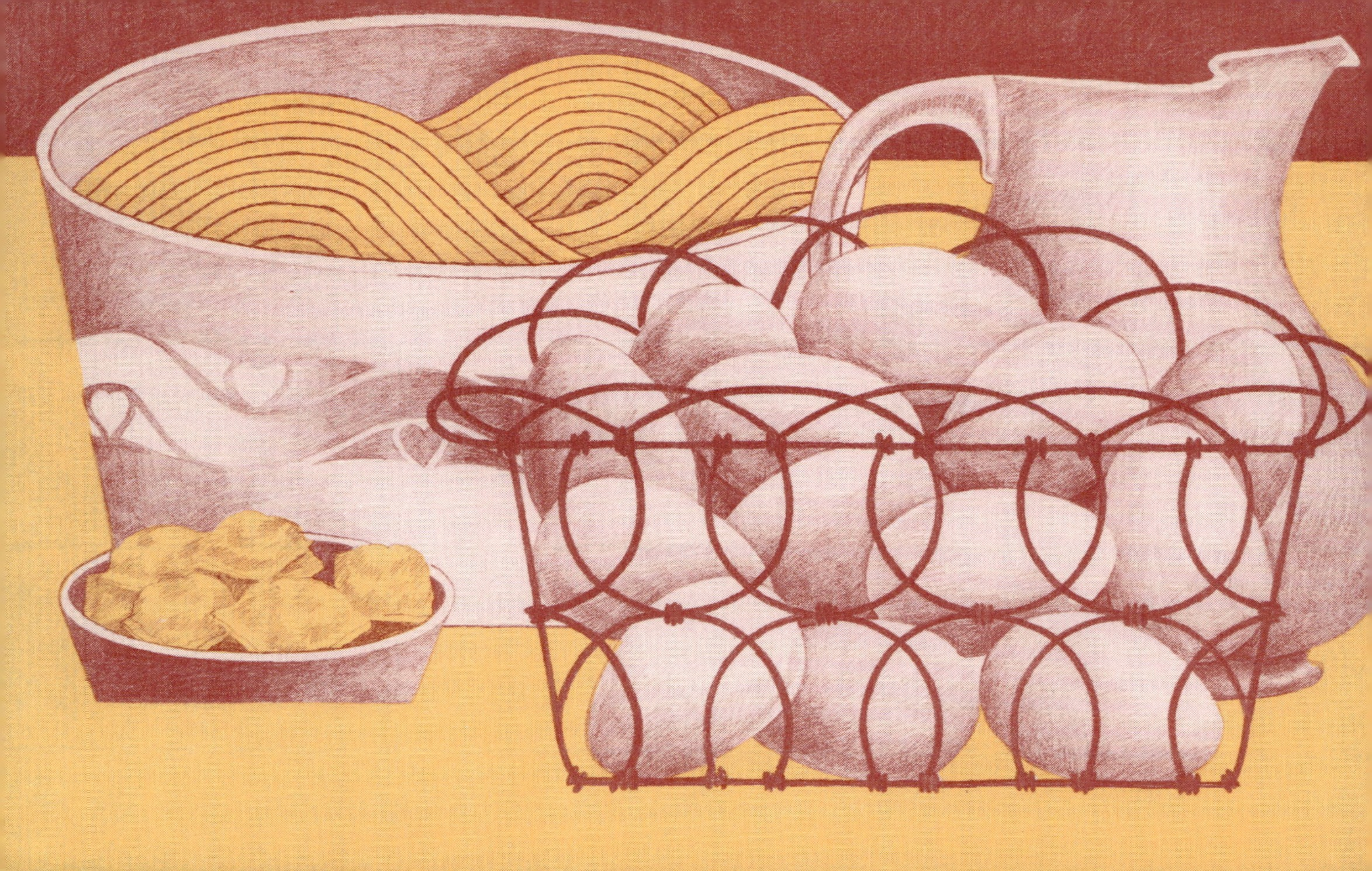

# PASTA

Pasta is shaped into a wide variety of forms and is used in many different cuisines. It includes all forms of macaroni, spaghetti and noodles. Orientals use thick and thin noodles and won ton squares; egg noodles are widely used in Germany, and Eastern Europeans frequently use noodles in place of potatoes. Italians love their pasta in dozens of shapes and sizes.

Pasta is a dough made of flour and water to which eggs, oil, pureed vegetables or herbs are added for variety. It can be generally divided into four different classifications. A few examples of each are listed below.

**Long thin pasta —** including vermicelli, spaghetti, spaghettini and fusilli.

**Hollow pasta —** macaroni, ziti, rigatoni and large hollow pastas such as manicotti which are stuffed before baking.

**Flat pasta —** egg noodles, linguini, lasagne and fettucini. Flat pasta is also made into ravioli, tortellini and cannelloni.

**Fancy pasta —** includes all sizes and shapes of decorative pasta such as wagon wheels, sea shells, bowties and butterflies.

Pasta can be boiled, baked, stuffed, sauced and deep fried. It combines well with vegetables, fish, meats, cheeses and eggs. It is used in soups, appetizers, main courses

and even in sweet desserts. Pasta is nutritious and low in fat and when made with eggs or oil it provides protein and energy-giving carbohydrates. It is an economical and satisfying food, and one pound of pasta prepared as a main dish will serve at least four people.

A steaming plate of freshly cooked pasta, dressed simply with butter and cheese or a thick savory sauce, is a delicious dish. Your own homemade pasta will be even more of a taste treat, and making it can be as satisfying as baking bread. This is not the formidable process you might imagine. One pound of fresh pasta can be made in less than an hour. A handcranked or electric pasta machine is helpful and fun to use, but whether you make the pasta by hand or with a machine, its texture and flavor will add to any dish that is being prepared.

Included in this book are simple instructions for making and cooking your own pasta if you are so inclined, however all of the recipes may also be prepared with the packaged variety.

The different pasta shapes suggested in the recipes which follow should be considered as only a starting point. With the wide variety of pastas available it is possible to give your favorite dishes a new look every time you prepare them. We suggest that you

experiment and concoct your own favorite combinations of pastas and sauces.

This is a short, but by no means complete description of some of the pasta types available.

**Agnolotti** — Round ravioli usually stuffed with a meat filling.
**Bucatini** — Hollow pasta tubes, a little thicker than spaghetti.

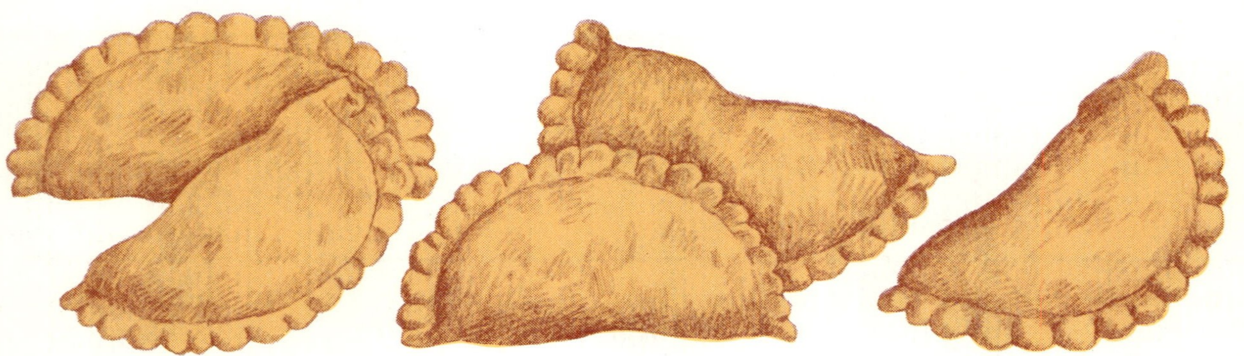

**Cannelloni** — Large hollow tubes or squares of sheet pasta, stuffed, rolled into cylinders and baked.

**Cappelletti** — Called "little hats" because of their round cap shape. They are stuffed like ravioli.

**Conchiglie** — Also called "sea shells." Fluted shell shaped pasta either ridged or smooth. Available in many sizes. The larger sizes can be stuffed.

**Farfalle** — Butterfly or bowshaped pasta available in many sizes.

**Fettuccini** — Ribbon noodles about 1/4-inch wide, served with a wide variety of sauces, the most familiar being Fettuccini Alfredo.

**Fusilli** — Spiral shaped spaghetti strands.

**Gnocchi** — A small fluted pasta shell, or a small dumpling made of flour, semolina or potatoes.

**Lasagne** — A wide flat noodle with straight or curly edges, baked in layers with meat or vegetable filling.

**Linguine** — Very narrow flat noodles.

**Macaroni** — This is the Italian word for all dried pasta. The common usage means pasta tubes, which can be short, long, thick, thin, curved or straight.

**Manicotti** — Either a large 4-inch long, 1-inch diameter tube, or a square of flat pasta which is stuffed, rolled into a cylinder and baked.

**Noodles** — Ribbons of flat pasta available in widths ranging from 1/8-inch to over 1-inch.

**Orecchiette** — Small ear-shaped pieces of pasta.
**Pansotti** — A stuffed dumpling similar to ravioli, usually triangular in shape.
**Ravioli** — A well-known square pasta dumpling stuffed with various meat, cheese or vegetable fillings.

**Rigatoni** — Hollow macaroni tubes about 1/2-inch in diameter and 2 inches long.
**Spaghetti** — Thin, solid round pasta strings, any length.
**Spaghettini** — A thinner variety of spaghetti.
**Rote** — Wheel-shaped pasta.
**Tagliatelle** — Flat egg noodles approximately 1/2-inch to 5/8-inch wide.
**Tagliarini** — A thinner version of Tagliatelle.
**Tortellini** — Small ring or half moon shaped stuffed pasta.
**Trenette** — Genoa name for a narrower and thicker tagliatelle noodle.
**Tubetti** — Short tubular pasta, approximately 1/4-inch diameter and 1/2-inch long, also known as salad macaroni.
**Tubettini** — Shorter version of tubetti, approximately 1/4-inch long.
**Vermicelli and Vermicellini** — Very thin spaghetti, sometimes sold in curled or cluster form. Also the names for spaghetti and spaghettini in Naples and Southern Italy.
**Ziti** — Smaller and smoother type of rigatoni, about 1/2-inch thick.

There are many small shapes generally used in soups called **pastina, capellini, stellette,** etc.

FLOUR

# MAKING YOUR OWN PASTA

Making pasta is similar to baking bread. It is a creative and satisfying experience to turn out lovely long straight noodles, and then cook and sauce them. Fresh pasta tastes better than packaged, partly because you made it.

Invite some friends into your kitchen for a pasta making session and plan to eat the fresh pasta for dinner afterwards. With a few extra hands it is possible to make several kinds of pasta and sauces in a short time. Make spinach pasta and a plain pasta, and one or two special sauces. Serve a crisp salad or marinated vegetables, warm bread and a favorite wine to complete a delicious dinner.

Here are some easy recipes for making pasta either by hand or machine.

# HOMEMADE PASTA

2 cups flour
3 eggs
1/2 tsp. salt
2 tbs. olive oil
1 to 2 tbs. water

**To make pasta by hand,** place a dome of flour on the counter or mixing surface. Make a well in flour. Break eggs into well. Add salt and olive oil. With a kitchen fork gently stir a little of the flour from the edges into the eggs. Continue stirring until eggs and flour are fairly well combined and mixture is too stiff to continue stirring with a fork. Gently knead in the rest of the flour by hand, adding as much water as necessary to incorporate all of the flour. The dough should be smooth and elastic after kneading, similar to bread dough. Let dough rest 10 to 15 minutes at room temperature then divide dough into two or three pieces. Dust a heavy rolling pin with flour and roll one piece of dough at a time on a lightly floured surface. Cover the remaining dough with a damp paper towel to keep it from drying out. Roll dough into a large thin circle by continuing to roll from the center to the edges. When the dough is approximately 1/8-inch

thick, make a final rolling to make the dough paper thin. To do this stretch the pasta dough sideways with your hands while you roll back and forth with the rolling pin. Start with the far edge of the dough and lay about a fourth of the circle over the rolling pin. As you are rolling it towards you, quickly slide your hands out to the ends of the rolling pin, gently stretching the pasta away from the center while you roll the rolling pin back and forth very rapidly. Turn the pin 90 degrees, cover it with another quarter of the dough, and repeat the process. Continue until the whole circle of dough has been stretched. Repeat the rolling and stretching until the dough is paper thin and almost transparent. Do not roll each piece more than 10 minutes or the dough may become dry and lose its elasticity. Repeat the rolling and stretching process with the remaining pieces of dough. Let the dough rest for a few minutes before cutting into noodles. Place a clean towel on the counter, allowing about one-third of the towel to hang over the edge. Place the pasta circle on the towel, with approximately one-third of the pasta hanging over the side. Turn circle every 10 minutes. The dough will dry in approximately 30 minutes. The pasta is ready to cut when it is dry to touch and looks slightly leathery. Drying the dough before cutting will help prevent the cut noodles from sticking together. Roll the dry, but still pliable dough, into a flat jelly roll shape, approx-

imately 3-inches wide. Cut the pasta with a sharp knife to the desired width. **Fettuccini** is cut approximately 1/4-inch wide; **noodles** can range from 1/8-inch to 1-inch; **tagliarini** is cut approximately 1/8-inch wide; **pappardelle** are broad noodles approximately 3/4-inch wide, cut with a fluted cutter; **lasagne** is cut 1-inch wide or wider, or can be cut in squares; **manicotti and cannelloni wrappers** are made by cutting fresh pasta in 3 or 4-inch squares. The squares are cooked and then wrapped around a filling to form a cylinder.

The cut pasta is now ready to be cooked, or it can be dried completely at room temperature and stored for later use. Sprinkle with a little flour to prevent sticking together while drying.

**Homemade Pasta with a Heavy Duty Mixer:** Place all ingredients in basic recipe on page 10 in mixing bowl. Beat with paddle attachment or kneading hook until dough forms a ball and cleans sides of mixing bowl. Let rest 15 to 20 minutes and roll out by hand or with pasta machine.

**Making Pasta with Pasta Machine:** Make pasta dough using the basic recipe on page 10. Divide dough into two or three pieces and knead by machine instead of by hand. This is done by setting the pasta machine rollers at highest setting. Run dough through machine until it becomes very smooth and pliable. Fold dough into thirds each time before putting through the machine again for easier handling. Change to next lower setting. Run dough through this setting one or two times. Continue until you reach the next to lowest setting. Stop at this point if you are making very narrow noodles; if you are making wide noodles go to the lowest setting. Attach the handle to either the wide or narrow cutting rollers. Lightly flour the rolled dough and cut it into the length you want your finished noodles to be before putting it through the cutters.

**Electric Pasta Machine:** There is an electric pasta machine on the market, made in Italy, which operates in the same way as the hand-cranked pasta machine. The dough is kneaded at the widest setting to the next to lowest setting. Use the lowest set-

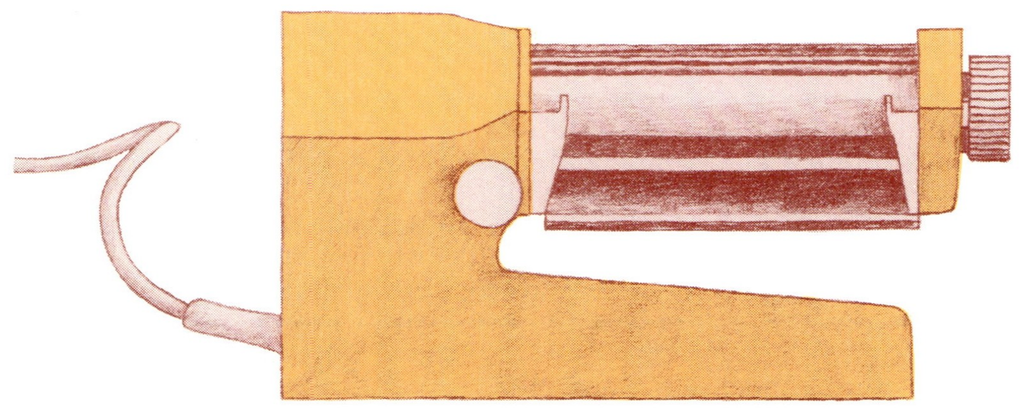

ting only if you are making won ton squares or fila dough. The lowest setting produces an extremely thin dough.

**Cleaning the Pasta Machine:** It is important that you **never** wash your pasta machine. It should be carefully cleaned with a soft brush. The dried particles will fall out easily.

**Cooking Pasta:** Start with a large deep kettle. Use approximately 6 quarts of water and 3 tablespoons salt for each pound of pasta. Bring water to a full rolling boil, and keep it boiling while pasta is cooking. It is not necessary to break long pasta as it will soften and slide into the water. Do not overcook pasta. It should be firm to the bite, but not too chewy. Dried homemade pasta takes 5 to 6 minutes. Fresh homemade pasta is usually done in 3 to 4 minutes. Commercial dried pasta generally takes 10 to 15 minutes to cook. Follow the package cooking times for each variety. A good indicator that the pasta is almost done is when it rises to the top of the water. Do not stir the pasta with a spoon while it is cooking because this can cause the pieces to stick together. Use a long handled fork for a quick stir once or twice during the cooking. Drain pasta into a large colander. Have a hot serving dish ready. Pour into serving dish and serve immediately.

# PASTA WITH SEMOLINA FLOUR

Pasta with semolina flour is much easier to make with a pasta machine, as the dough is quite stiff and almost impossible to roll to the desired thinness by hand. Semolina produces a nice texture and the pasta is less fragile to handle. It helps to let the dough rest an hour before kneading and rolling to allow the flour to expand. Semolina has the texture of granulated sugar, is light yellow in color, and can be obtained in Italian and food specialty markets.

1 cup all purpose flour
1 cup semolina
2 eggs
1 tsp. salt
1 tbs. olive oil
2 to 3 tbs. water

Place all ingredients in mixing bowl of a heavy duty mixer. Use paddle or kneading hook to mix until dough forms a ball and cleans sides of bowl. Let rest covered with plastic wrap at least an hour before rolling and cutting with a pasta machine.

# CARROT PASTA

Pasta can be made in a variety of flavors. Pureed vegetables such as carrots or spinach add color as well as flavor. This dough is soft enough to make by hand.

1/2 cup carrot puree (2 to 3 carrots)
2-1/2 cups flour
3 eggs
2 tbs. olive oil
1/2 tsp. salt
1 to 2 tbs. water as necessary

Peel and cook carrots until very soft. Puree in blender or food processor. Press puree through a sieve to remove any remaining pieces. Measure out 1/2 cup puree and return to saucepan. Cook for a minute or two over very low heat to dry out as much as possible. Combine puree with remaining ingredients and continue as directed in basic recipe on page 10.

Variation: Use 1/2 cup spinach puree and a pinch of nutmeg in place of carrots.

SOY
SAUCE

# PASTA SAUCES

A sauce can make good pasta perfect. All pastas are complemented by the addition of a sauce. It may be a simple one of melted butter, cream and freshly grated cheese, or a favorite one easily assembled in minutes while the pasta is cooking, or a special sauce which needs hours of simmering.

Pasta sauces vary in flavor from subtle to spicy. The blandness of pasta enables it to blend perfectly with either. In this chapter we have included a sampling of sauces using a variety of ingredients including shrimp, clams, nuts, cheese, vegetables, chicken, sausage, fresh basil leaves and pine nuts.

After you have tried our recipes, blend your own favorite combinations into original pasta sauces.

The amount of pasta for a serving and how much sauce to put on it is an individual preference. In general, 8 ounces of uncooked pasta will make 3 medium size servings, or 6 first course servings.

# CREAMY SHRIMP SAUCE

Serve this sauce with small pasta shells or spaghettini.

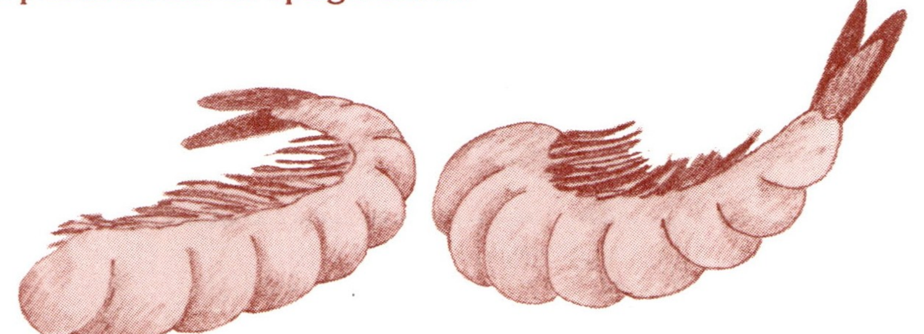

1-1/2 cups sour cream
1/4 cup heavy cream
1 tbs. soy sauce
1 tsp. Worcestershire sauce
1/2 tsp. dry mustard
1 tsp. dried dill weed
1/4 tsp. white pepper
1/2 lb. small cooked shrimp

Heat sour cream, heavy cream, soy sauce, Worcestershire, dry mustard, dill weed and pepper until just heated through. Add shrimp to sauce and heat until shrimp are hot. Toss with hot cooked pasta and serve immediately. Makes sauce for 6 first course servings or 4 luncheon or supper servings using 8 ounces cooked, well-drained pasta.

# WHITE CLAM SAUCE

Clams cooked with white wine and garlic make a delicious quick pasta sauce.

1/4 cup butter
1 large clove garlic, minced
2 tbs. flour
2 cans (6-1/2 ozs. ea.) chopped clams
1/4 cup white wine or dry vermouth
1/4 cup parsley, finely chopped
1/2 tsp. thyme
salt and pepper

Melt butter in small saucepan. Add garlic and cook one minute. Stir in flour and cook two minutes. Drain clams, reserving juice. Combine reserved clam juice and white wine. Add enough water to make 2 cups liquid. Add to flour mixture and cook until sauce thickens slightly. Add parsley, salt, pepper and thyme. Simmer for approximately 10 minutes. Add clams and heat through. Makes sauce for one pound cooked, well-drained pasta—enough for 4 to 5 servings.

# CLAM SAUCE WITH TOMATOES

This sauce is particularly nice served with small pasta shells. You may substitute any firm fleshed fish such as halibut or rock cod for the clams.

1 can (28 ozs.) Italian style tomatoes
2 cans (6-1/2 ozs. ea.) chopped or minced clams
1 can (8 ozs.) tomato sauce
1/4 cup dry vermouth or dry table wine
2 tsp. sugar
1-1/2 tsp. sweet basil
1 tsp. marjoram
1 tbs. olive oil
1 clove garlic, cut in half
1 small onion, finely chopped
1/4 cup finely chopped green pepper
salt and pepper to taste
1 tsp. cornstarch

Empty tomatoes into sieve over a bowl. Cut tomatoes in half. Squeeze out most of the seeds. Trim away hard core and chop tomatoes coarsely. Put strained juice and chopped tomatoes in saucepan. Drain juice from canned clams and set clams aside. Add clam juice, tomato sauce, vermouth, sugar, basil and marjoram to tomatoes. Bring to boil. Cook over medium heat, stirring occasionally. Heat olive oil in small skillet. Saute garlic until light brown. Remove and discard. Add onion and green pep-

per to skillet. Saute until onion is transparent. Add onion and green pepper to simmering sauce. Season with salt and pepper to taste. Continue to cook for approximately 15 minutes until sauce thickens. Dissolve cornstarch in one tablespoon of cold water. Stir into sauce and cook for a few minutes. Add reserved clams and heat through. Makes sauce for one pound of cooked, well-drained pasta—enough for 4 or 5 servings.

Note: If fish is substituted for the clams, lightly flour the fish and saute in 2 to 3 tablespoons olive oil. Cut into cubes and add to tomato sauce. Cook approximately 10 minutes before serving. Increase vermouth or wine to 1/2 cup and omit clam juice.

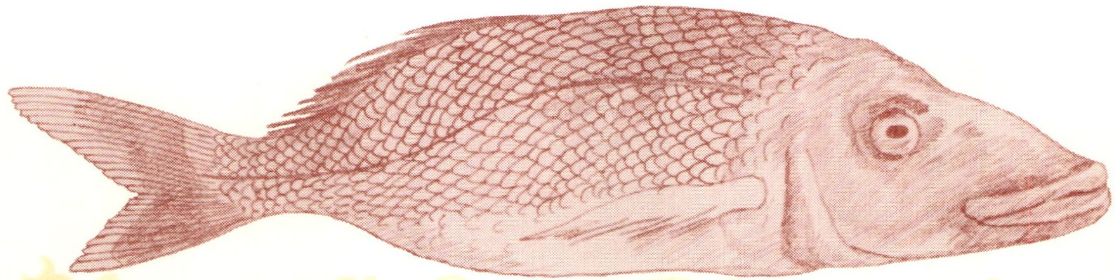

# SAVORY CHICKEN SAUCE

5 tbs. olive oil
1 medium onion, finely chopped
1 clove garlic, minced
1 can (16 ozs.) S&W Diced Tomatoes in Rich Puree
1 can (8 ozs.) tomato sauce
1/4 bay leaf
1/4 tsp. **each** thyme, marjoram and oregano
1 tsp. tarragon
1 tsp. beef extract (Bovril)
1/4 cup dry sherry or white wine
2 tbs. brandy
2 cups cooked cubed chicken (1/2 to 3/4-inch cubes)
1/2 lb. fresh mushrooms, sliced
salt and pepper to taste

Heat 2 tablespoons olive oil in a large skillet. Add onion and garlic. Cook over low heat until onion is soft. Add tomatoes, tomato sauce, bay leaf, thyme, marjoram,

oregano, tarragon, beef extract, sherry and brandy. Cover and cook over low heat 15 minutes to blend flavors. Add chicken, salt and pepper. Cook covered 15 minutes. Heat remaining olive oil in skillet. Saute fresh mushrooms 4 to 5 minutes. Add to sauce just before serving over broad noodles. Makes sauce for 8 ounces of pasta, cooked as directed and drained well—enough for 3 to 4 servings.

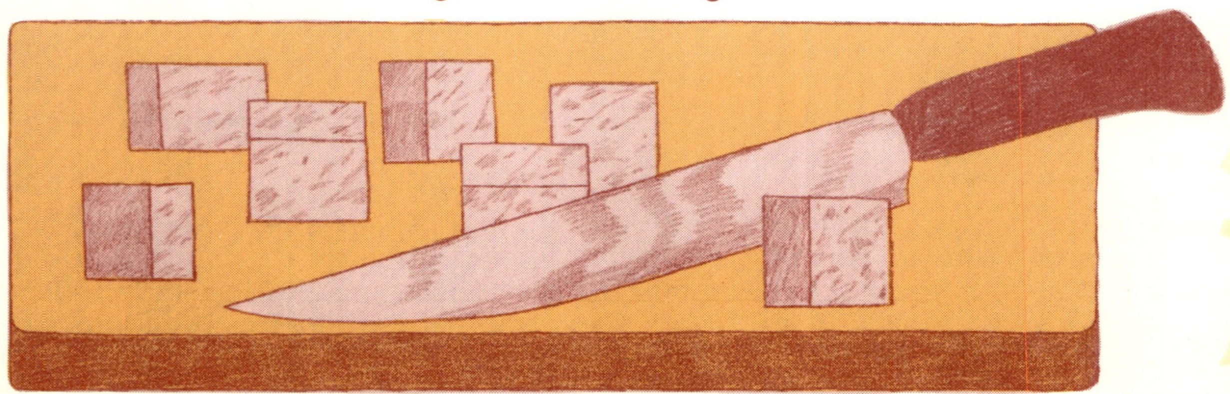

# MEAT SAUCE

This is a fresh tasting sauce to make when tomatoes are out of season

1 can (1 lb. 12 ozs.) Italian style tomatoes
2 tbs. tomato paste
1 can (8 ozs.) tomato sauce
2 tsp. sugar
1 tbs. sweet basil
1/2 tsp. marjoram
1/2 cup dry vermouth or white wine
1/2 tsp. salt
1/4 tsp. pepper
1/2 lb. ground beef
1 small onion, finely chopped
1 clove garlic, minced
1/4 cup chopped green pepper
1 tbs. olive oil
6 to 8 fresh mushrooms, sliced

Drain tomatoes in a sieve over a bowl. Cut tomatoes in half and squeeze out most of the seeds. Trim out any hard stem at the base of the tomatoes. Chop tomatoes coarsely. Put strained tomato juice and chopped tomato in a large saucepan. Bring to boil. Add tomato paste, tomato sauce, sugar, sweet basil, marjoram, vermouth, salt and pepper. Simmer over very low heat, stirring occasionally. Brown ground beef in a skillet. Break into small pieces with spatula while it cooks. Using a slotted spoon,

remove ground beef from skillet and add to tomato mixture. Pour all but one tablespoon of fat out of skillet. Add onions, garlic and green pepper and saute until soft. Add to tomato sauce. Heat olive oil in skillet. Saute mushrooms 4 to 5 minutes. Add to sauce. Simmer uncovered 25 to 30 minutes. Makes sauce for one pound of pasta cooked as directed and drained well—enough for 4 to 5 servings.

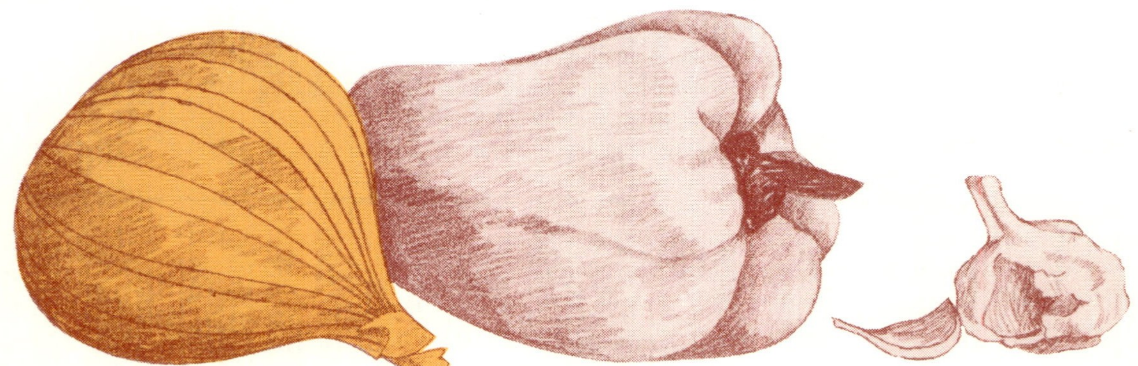

# MEATBALL SAUCE

Here is an old fashioned meatball and tomato sauce for pasta.

1 lb. ground chuck
2 eggs
2 tbs. finely chopped parsley
1/4 cup finely chopped onion
2 tbs. grated Parmesan cheese
1 tsp. salt
1/2 tsp. pepper
10 soda crackers, crumbled

1/3 cup olive oil
1/4 cup chopped onion
1 clove garlic, minced
1 can (14 ozs.) Italian style tomatoes
1 can (8 ozs.) tomato sauce
1 can (10-1/4 ozs.) beef gravy
1 tsp. Italian herb seasoning
1/2 tsp. salt

In large mixing bowl combine ground chuck, eggs, parsley, onion, Parmesan cheese, 1 teaspoon salt, pepper, and soda crackers. Mix well. Shape into 1-1/2 to 2-inch meatballs. Heat olive oil in large skillet. Brown meatballs on all sides. Remove from skillet and set aside. Pour all but one tablespoon oil from pan. Saute chopped onion and garlic in oil until soft. Scrape up brown bits from bottom of skillet. Add tomatoes with their juice, tomato sauce, beef gravy, herb seasoning, 1/2 teaspoon salt and pep-

per to taste. Bring to boil. Return meatballs to skillet. Reduce heat to very low and simmer meatballs in sauce, uncovered, for 25 to 30 minutes. Makes sauce for one pound pasta cooked as directed and drained well—enough for 4 to 5 servings.

LAYNE

# PEPPERONI AND MUSHROOM SAUCE

This is a quick sauce you can put together while the pasta is cooking

1 tbs. oil
1/4 lb. pepperoni, skin removed and thinly sliced
1/2 lb. fresh mushrooms, thinly sliced
1/2 tsp. salt
4 to 5 green onions
1/2 cup heavy cream

Heat oil in large skillet. Saute pepperoni 3 to 4 minutes. Add sliced mushrooms, salt and onions. Saute 4 to 5 minutes until mushrooms are done. Add cream and heat through. Pour sauce over hot cooked pasta. Makes sauce for 8 ounces of pasta cooked as directed and drained well—enough for 3 to 4 servings.

# SPICY SAUSAGE SAUCE

1/4 cup dried mushrooms (optional)
2 tbs. olive oil
1 medium onion, chopped
1 green pepper, chopped
1 stalk celery, diced
1 clove garlic, minced
1 can (1 lb. 14 ozs.) Italian style tomatoes
**or** 2 lbs. fresh tomatoes
1 can (14 ozs.) tomato puree
1 can (14 ozs.) Swanson's beef broth
1/2 cup red wine
1/2 tsp. rosemary
1/2 tsp. oregano
1/4 tsp. fennel seeds
1 bay leaf
1/8 tsp. red pepper flakes
1/2 tsp. salt
4 to 6 mild or hot Italian sausages

Cover dried mushrooms with warm water and set aside. Heat olive oil in a large heavy pot. Saute onion, pepper, celery, and garlic until soft but not brown. Chop tomatoes and discard hard cores. Add tomatoes with their juice, tomato puree, beef broth, red wine, rosemary, oregano, fennel, bay leaf, red pepper flakes and salt. Drain dried mushrooms and squeeze dry. Add to sauce. Simmer sauce uncovered for approximately 45 minutes. Place sausages in a skillet. Add 1/2 cup water and cover. Simmer

15 minutes. Drain off water and brown sausages. Cut into 1/2-inch slices. Add to sauce. Simmer for another 15 minutes. Makes sauce for 1-1/2 pounds pasta cooked as directed and drained well—enough for 6 servings.

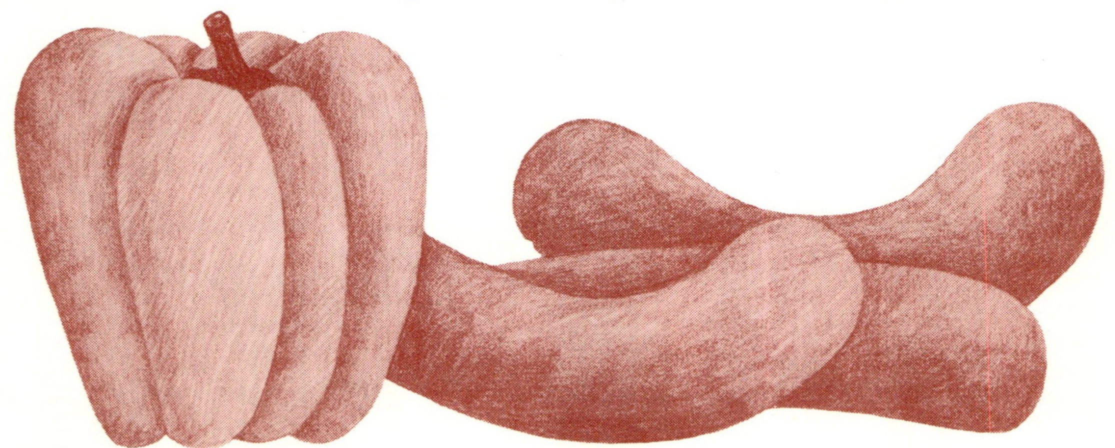

# MUSHROOM SAUCE

This sauce combines fresh and Oriental dried mushrooms. Serve over Chinese noodles or your favorite pasta.

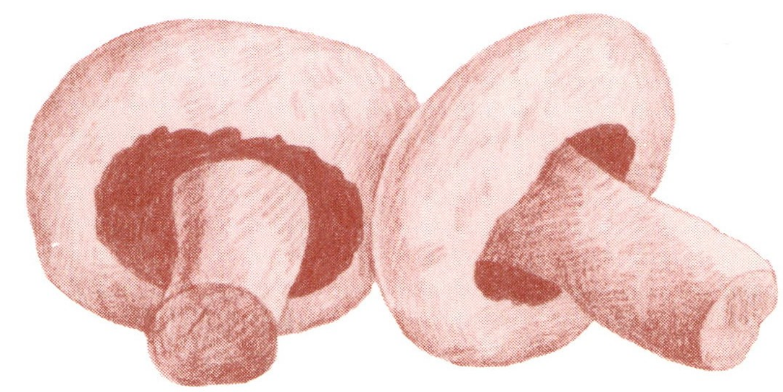

4 large dried Oriental mushrooms
1/4 cup butter
1 lb. fresh mushrooms, thickly sliced
3 tbs. minced shallots
1 garlic clove, minced
1 can (14 ozs.) Swanson's beef broth
2 tsp. Worcestershire sauce
4 tsp. cornstarch
1/3 cup dry sherry
1 tbs. soy sauce
white pepper

Cover dried mushrooms with warm water for approximately 15 minutes. Drain, squeeze fairly dry and chop coarsely. Melt butter in large skillet. When foaming add

sliced mushrooms. Saute over high heat 2 to 3 minutes. Add shallots, garlic and softened dried mushrooms. Cook 2 more minutes. Add beef broth and Worcestershire. Dissolve cornstarch in sherry. Stir cornstarch mixture into mushrooms. Cook until sauce thickens. Add soy sauce and pepper. Serve over hot cooked pasta. Makes sauce for one pound of pasta cooked as directed and drained well—enough for 4 servings.

# FOUR-CHEESE SAUCE

Four favorite cheeses are combined with cream and seasonings for an easy and delicious sauce.

1 tsp. butter
1 garlic clove, mashed
1/2 cup whipping cream
1/4 cup Parmesan cheese
1/2 cup grated Gruyere or Swiss cheese
1/4 cup cream cheese
1/4 cup blue veined cheese
1/2 tsp. white pepper
1/2 tsp. salt
nutmeg

Melt butter in small saucepan. Saute garlic clove until it starts to turn color. Remove garlic and discard. Add cream, Parmesan, Gruyere, cream cheese and blue cheese to saucepan. Cook over very low heat, stirring constantly until cheeses melt. Add pepper, salt and a dash of nutmeg. Serve over hot pasta. Makes sauce for one pound of pasta cooked as directed and drained well—enough for 4 to 5 servings.

# NUT SAUCE

Serve over small shells or bowties or with the Cheese Ravioli, page 47.

2 tbs. butter
1 large clove garlic, minced
2 tbs. flour
1-1/3 cups Swanson's beef or chicken broth
1/2 tsp. anchovy paste
1/4 tsp. white pepper
1/4 tsp. salt
1 cup walnuts, very finely chopped
1/3 cup heavy cream

Melt butter in small saucepan. Saute garlic for one minute. Add flour and cook 2 minutes. Gradually add broth, anchovy paste, pepper and salt. Cook until sauce thickens. Stir in walnuts and cream just before serving. Cook just long enough to heat sauce. Makes sauce for 8 ounces of pasta cooked as directed and drained well—enough for 3 to 4 servings.

# PESTO SAUCE

Fragrant fresh sweet basil leaves, garlic and pine nuts make a delicious sauce for one recipe of homemade pasta.

1-1/2 to 2 cups fresh basil leaves
1 cup fresh spinach leaves
1/2 cup olive oil
2 cloves garlic
1 tsp. salt
2 tbs. pine nuts or almonds
3/4 cups freshly grated Parmesan cheese
homemade pasta, page 10
2 tbs. butter (for pasta)

Place fresh basil, spinach leaves, olive oil, salt, garlic and nuts in blender container. Blend at high speed. Scrape down sides. Continue blending until mixture is fairly smooth. Pour into bowl and stir in grated cheese. Cook pasta and drain well. Place in warm bowl. Add butter and quickly toss to blend. Pour pesto sauce over pasta and gently mix. Makes 6 first course servings.

# ZUCCHINI TOMATO SAUCE

This is a quick garden fresh sauce for spaghetti or shells.

2 tbs. butter
1 medium onion, chopped
1 garlic clove, minced
3 medium zucchini
1 can (15 ozs.) tomato sauce
with tomato tidbits

1/2 tsp. marjoram
1/2 tsp. oregano
1/2 tsp. sweet basil
1/2 tsp. salt
1/4 tsp. white pepper

Melt butter in medium saucepan. Saute onion until soft but not brown. Add minced garlic. Trim zucchini. Slice in half lengthwise then slice across in 1/4 to 1/2-inch slices. Add to softened onion and garlic. Stir in tomato sauce, marjoram, oregano, sweet basil, salt and pepper. Cover and simmer 15 to 20 minutes, stirring occasionally. Makes sauce for one pound pasta cooked as directed and drained well—enough for 4 servings.

# PASTA SPECIALTIES

Homemade ravioli with a wide variety of delicious fillings are fun to make and professional results can be achieved with an inexpensive ravioli mold or an individual ravioli stamp.

Cannelloni, manicotti, and lasagne also make excellent appetizers or entrees, and are ideal for pot luck or cooperative dinners. They can be made ahead and refrigerated for a day or two, or frozen, if you aren't going to use them immediately.

Included in this section are directions for making ravioli and two delicious fillings, plus other pasta specialties using fresh vegetables, cheese, sausage and chicken. Consider using jumbo shells in place of manicotti or cannelloni shells to give old favorites a new look.

# HOMEMADE RAVIOLI

Ravioli are little squares or circles of flat pasta filled with meat, cheese or spinach, and served with a sauce or melted butter and cheese. They can be made with a ravioli form which turns out 10 or 12 at a time, or they can be stamped out individually with a single ravioli cutter or a round cookie cutter, or they can be made freeform on a large sheet of pasta using a kitchen knife to cut the squares. There is also a slotted or ridged rolling pin which marks the filled ravioli squares for cutting.

Start by preparing your filling, then refrigerate it so that it has a chance to stiffen for easier handling. This step is particularly important if you are using a cheese filling made with ricotta cheese. Make your pasta dough—using the basic homemade pasta recipe on page 10. Roll out the dough as thinly as possible. Do not let it dry, because it becomes difficult to fill and cut. Cover the portion of dough not being used with a damp towel to prevent it from drying out.

**If you are using a ravioli form,** cut the dough into strips approximately one-inch wider and one-inch longer than the form. If it is a two-part form, flour the metal frame and place one strip of dough over the top. Place the other half of the form which has small indentations in it, directly on top of the pasta dough. Press down lightly to mark filling depressions, and remove form. Place a small amount of filling, usually 1/2 to 1

teaspoon depending on size of the ravioli, in each depression. Overfilling may cause them to break open during cooking. Brush edges of each ravioli with a little water. A pastry brush works well for this. Place another strip of dough over top of filling. Gently press down dough along ridges of the ravioli form. With a heavy rolling pin, roll across ravioli form two or three times to cut dough into individual squares. They will not come completely apart with this rolling. Gently turn ravioli out of the form, flat side down onto a floured cookie sheet. Cover with a towel and let rest an hour before cooking. As the ravioli dry they will break apart easily.

**If you are using a single ravioli or cookie cutter,** cut as many squares or circles as possible out of the dough. Place a small amount of filling on half of the squares or circles. Brush edges with a little water. Place another square or circle directly on top of filling and firmly press each ravioli around the edges. Place on a floured cookie sheet or plate, cover with a towel, and let rest an hour before cooking. Ravioli will expand in size during cooking, so if you have a large cutter you may wish to make triangles or half circles from one piece of cut dough rather than using two pieces to form the ravioli.

**To make ravioli without a form,** cut a straight line across the top of dough with

a knife or fluted pastry cutter. Place small amounts of filling approximately 1-1/2 inches apart, 2-1/2 inches down from the cut edge. Brush dough with a little water in a straight line below filling and in between the fillings, making square outlines. Fold down cut edge over filling. Press down firmly along bottom edge of folded over pasta dough and then cut out individual ravioli as uniformly as possible. Using a fork, press edges together well to be sure a good seal is formed. Using the bottom line you have just cut for the top of the dough, continue placing filling 1-1/2 inches apart, 2-1/2 inches down from the top edge, and repeat the moistening and cutting process until you have used all the filling. Place ravioli on a floured cookie sheet or plate, cover, and let rest an hour before cooking. After raviolis are made, they may be frozen or refrigerated prior to cooking.

**To cook ravioli** bring 6 to 8 quarts of water to a rapid boil. Add 1 tablespoon salt. Drop in ravioli and cook for 10 to 12 minutes, depending on thickness of dough and size. Drain well and pour into a heated bowl. Cover with sauce or melted butter and Parmesan cheese. Serve immediately.

If desired, cooked ravioli can be added to beef or chicken broth and served as a hearty soup.

**Ravioli fillings** can be made with a wide variety of foods. Chicken, leftover roast beef, veal, clams, spinach and cheese used alone or in combinations make good fillings. Cooked meat should be minced or ground and then seasoned and mixed with beaten egg to hold the filling together. Classic ravioli fillings tend to be very lightly seasoned so they are complemented with flavorful tomato sauces or pesto. Try making fillings and sauces with your favorite foods.

Here are two of our favorite ravioli fillings, one using chicken, and the other a savory cheese mixture. Try cheese ravioli with Nut Sauce, page 37, or Pesto, page 38.

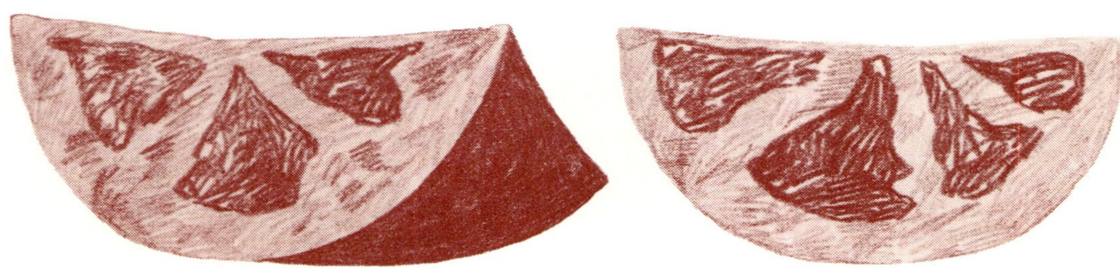

# CHICKEN AND SAUSAGE FILLING

1-1/2 cups diced cooked chicken
1 mild or hot Italian sausage, cooked
1 egg
3 tbs. chopped parsley
1/2 tsp. salt
1/4 tsp. pepper
1/2 tsp. Worcestershire sauce
1/4 cup Parmesan cheese

Put chicken and sausage through meat grinder twice, or chop very, very fine by hand or using food processor. Combine with egg, parsley, salt, pepper, Worcestershire and cheese. Refrigerate until you are ready to fill ravioli. Makes filling for approximately 4 dozen ravioli.

## CHEESE FILLING

1-1/2 cups ricotta cheese
1 cup grated Parmesan cheese
1/4 cup minced parsley
2 eggs
1/2 tsp. salt
1/4 tsp. white pepper
dash nutmeg
1/2 tsp. grated lemon rind

Combine all ingredients in a small bowl. Mix until smooth. Refrigerate until ready to fill ravioli.

# CANNELLONI

Fresh homemade pasta squares (see basic recipe on page 10) make the best cannelloni, but packaged manicotti tubes can be used if desired.

Chicken and Mushroom Filling, page 49
Tomato Sauce, page 50
Cheese Sauce, page 50
18 to 20 fresh pasta squares, page 13

If desired filling and sauces can be made ahead and refrigerated. When ready to use, warm sauces over low heat. Make pasta squares and cook immediately after cutting to prevent their drying out. Cook in rapidly boiling water about 8 minutes. Remove from water and cover with wet paper towels. To assemble cannelloni place 2 to 3 tablespoons of filling on the bottom third of each square. Roll into a cylinder. Place rolls seam side down in one large or 2 smaller well-buttered baking dishes. Spoon tomato sauce over rolls and top with cheese sauce. Bake at 350°F. 20 minutes until hot and bubbly. Cannelloni can be frozen before baking. Allow to defrost in refrigerator. Bake 35 to 40 minutes at 350°F. Cover with foil the first 20 minutes.

## CHICKEN AND MUSHROOM FILLING

4 to 5 tbs. olive oil
2 to 2-1/2 lbs. chicken thighs
1 large onion, finely chopped
2 carrots, finely chopped
1 clove garlic, minced
1 cup white wine
1/2 lb. fresh mushrooms
1/2 cup finely chopped parsley
1 egg
1 tsp. salt
1/2 tsp. pepper
1/2 cup Parmesan cheese

Remove skin from chicken. Heat 2 to 3 tablespoons oil in large skillet. Brown chicken on both sides. Remove from pan. Add onion, carrot and garlic to remaining oil in skillet. Saute until onion is soft. Scrape up brown bits from bottom of skillet. Return chicken pieces to skillet. Add wine. Bring to boil. Reduce heat and simmer covered 45 minutes. Remove from heat. When cool enough to handle remove chicken from bones. Heat remaining oil in another skillet. Saute mushrooms 4 to 5 minutes. Add mushrooms to chicken and put mixture through meat grinder, or chop in a food processor. Combine ground mixture with parsley, egg, salt, pepper and Parmesan.

## TOMATO SAUCE

1 tbs. olive oil
1/2 cup finely chopped onion
1 can (14 ozs.) Swanson's beef broth
1 can (14 ozs.) tomato puree
1 tsp. meat extract (Bovril)
1/4 cup Madeira or Marsala
1/2 tsp. oregano
1 tsp. sweet basil
1/2 tsp. sugar

Saute onion in olive oil until soft. Add remaining ingredients. Bring to boil. Cook uncovered over medium heat 20 to 25 minutes until sauce reduces and thickens.

## CHEESE SAUCE

3 tbs. **each** butter and flour
2 cups milk
1/2 cup Parmesan cheese
1 tsp. salt
1/4 tsp. white pepper
dash nutmeg

Melt butter in small saucepan. Stir in flour and cook 3 minutes. Gradually add milk. Cook until sauce thickens. Stir in remaining ingredients. Cook 3to 4 minutes.

# BROCCOLI AND CANADIAN BACON CANNELLONI

Cheese Sauce, page 53
1 tbs. butter
4 green onions, thinly sliced
1 cup diced Canadian bacon or cooked ham
1 cup ricotta cheese
4 tbs. Parmesan cheese
1 egg
1/2 tsp. salt
2 cups coarsely chopped cooked broccoli
8 manicotti shells

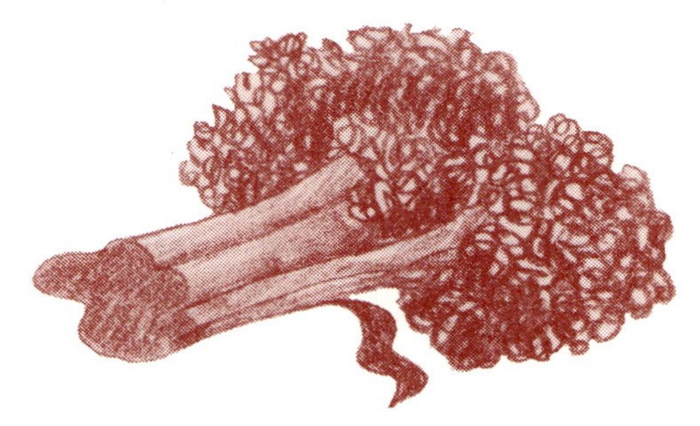

Prepare sauce as directed. Melt butter in small skillet. Saute onions for a minute or two to soften. Add Canadian bacon pieces and cook for another minute or two. In a small bowl combine ricotta, Parmesan, egg and salt. Mix well. Add bacon mixture, chopped broccoli and 1/2 cup cheese sauce. Cook pasta shells in boiling water 10 minutes. Drain well. Rinse in cold water for easier handling. Use a teaspoon or long handled iced tea spoon to stuff shells with filling. Place stuffed shells in buttered oven-

proof baking dish or individual au gratin dishes. Spoon remaining cheese sauce over shells. Bake in 350°F. oven 15 minutes, or until hot and bubbly. Place under broiler to lightly brown. Makes 4 servings of 2 cannelloni each.

**Variation:** 2 cups cooked chopped spinach may be substituted for broccoli.

## CHEESE SAUCE

3 tbs. butter
3 tbs. flour
2 cups milk
1-1/2 tsp. Worcestershire sauce
3/4 cup grated Swiss cheese
salt and pepper

Melt butter in small saucepan. Add flour and cook, stirring, for 2 minutes. Gradually add milk and Worcestershire sauce. Cook, stirring constantly, until sauce thickens. Add cheese, salt and pepper. Stir to blend. Use as directed.

# MANICOTTI

Cheese and spinach filled manicotti shells are topped with a zesty tomato sauce. Serve with a crisp salad and hot French bread.

3 tbs. butter
1 cup finely chopped onion
1 small clove garlic, minced
1 can (15 ozs.) tomato sauce
with tomato tidbits
1 tsp. sweet basil
1/2 tsp. oregano
salt and pepper
1/2 pkg. frozen chopped spinach

1-1/2 cups ricotta cheese
1 cup grated Swiss cheese
1/4 cup finely chopped parsley
1/2 tsp. salt
1/4 tsp. white pepper
4 to 6 drops Tabasco
dash nutmeg
8 packaged manicotti shells
Parmesan cheese for topping

Melt butter in saucepan. Saute onion and garlic until soft but not brown. Place one-half of mixture in mixing bowl. Set aside. To remaining onion in saucepan add tomato sauce, basil, oregano, salt and pepper. Simmer over low heat 20 to 25 minutes to blend flavors. Cook spinach according to package directions. Drain and squeeze as dry as

possible. Combine with reserved onion-garlic mixture. Add ricotta, Swiss cheese, parsley, salt, pepper, Tabasco and nutmeg. Mix well. Cook manicotti shells as directed on package. (If using stuff-a-roni shells, cook them for 6 minutes in large pot of boiling water. Drain and rinse with cold water for easier handling.) Stuff shells with cheese-spinach mixture using a teaspoon or iced-tea spoon. Place in a large buttered baking dish or individual au gratin dishes, allowing two shells per serving. Top with tomato sauce and sprinkle with Parmesan cheese. Bake in 375°F. oven for 20 minutes or until hot and bubbly. Makes 4 servings.

Note: This dish can be assembled ahead of time. Cover and refrigerate. Allow an extra 15 minutes baking time.

# LASAGNE

Meat Sauce, page 57
Cheese Sauce

homemade lasagne noodles, page 13
**or** 1 pkg. lasagne noodles

Prepare sauces as directed. Cook noodles and drain. Rinse with a little cold water for easier handling. Place one layer of cooked noodles in buttered 9 x 13-inch baking dish. Cover noodles with a layer of meat sauce. Cover meat sauce with layer of cheese sauce. Repeat layers. Finish with cheese sauce. Bake lasagne uncovered in a 325°F. oven until hot and bubbly, about 30 minutes. Let stand 10 minutes before serving. Makes 6 to 8 servings.

## CHEESE SAUCE

4 tbs. butter
1 small onion, chopped
3 tbs. flour
2 cups milk
3/4 cup grated Parmesan cheese
2 egg yolks

Melt butter in saucepan. Saute onion 2 to 3 minutes. Add flour and cook 2 minutes. Gradually add milk. Cook, stirring, until sauce thickens. Add Parmesan.

Blend a little sauce into egg yolks. Gradually add warmed egg yolks to sauce. Cook, over very low heat 10 minutes, stirring constantly.

## MEAT SAUCE

1-1/2 lbs. ground beef
1 large onion, chopped
1 clove garlic, minced
1/4 cup parsley, minced
1 can (28 ozs.) Italian style tomatoes
1 can (4 ozs.) tomato paste
1 bay leaf
1 tsp. salt
1/4 tsp. pepper
1 tsp. oregano
1/3 cup red wine

Brown beef in large skillet. Break into small pieces as it cooks. Drain off fat. Add onion, garlic and parsley. Cook until onion starts to soften. Add remaining ingredients. Break up large tomato pieces. Mix well. Simmer covered over low heat 45 minutes. If sauce seems thin, turn up heat for a few minutes.

# ORIENTAL PASTA DISHES

Although pasta was probably known in Italy long before Marco Polo returned from China, the Chinese have had several hundred years experience with both boiled and fried pasta. The basic Oriental pastas are Chinese noodles and won ton wrappers.

Chinese noodles are lighter in color and texture than Italian noodles. They are sometimes available fresh in one pound packages in the produce department of a market, or they can be found in dried form in the foreign specialty department. To substitute dried Chinese noodles for the fresh, cook one-half of the specified amount according to package directions. If totally unavailable, substitute spaghetti and cook one-half of the specified amount.

Won ton wrappers are thin squares of Chinese noodle dough measuring approximately 3 inches square. They are sold fresh in one pound packages in the produce section of some markets and are frequently found in the frozen food department. There are 60 to 80 won ton wrappers per pound, depending on thickness of the dough. Fresh wrappers will keep for a week or more in the refrigerator, or they can be frozen and defrosted when you are ready to use them. Fried won ton appetizers, can be made ahead and lightly browned in hot oil, cooled and then frozen in plastic containers. When you are ready to serve them, place on rack in a shallow pan and bake in a 350°F.

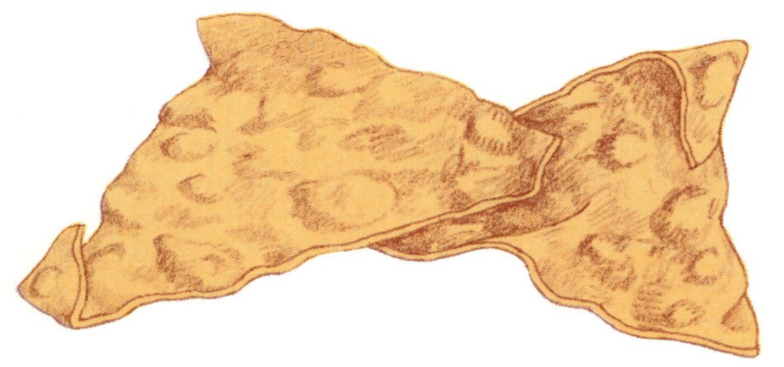

oven 10 to 15 minutes until hot and crisp.

Won ton for won ton soup are made in the same manner as the fried appetizers, except they are boiled in a rich broth until they are tender. They are served in a bowl with lots of the broth ladled over them.

Included in this section are recipes for a classic won ton to fry or to boil, a delicious Chinese noodle soup, a non-traditional Mexican type filling for won ton, and a Chinese New Year dessert won ton filled with peanuts and coconut which would be an easy cooking adventure for a child with a little adult help needed with the frying.

## CHINESE NOODLE SOUP

8 ozs. fresh Chinese-style noodles
**or** 4 ozs. dried noodles
2 cans (14 ozs. ea.) chicken broth or beef broth
1/2 tsp. sesame oil
1 tbs. soy sauce
white pepper
1/2 cup diced cooked ham, chicken, pork or shrimp
1/2 cup frozen peas
5 green onions with 1-inch of green top, thinly sliced

Cook noodles in large pot of rapidly boiling water for 3 minutes. Drain well. Bring chicken broth to boil in a large saucepan. Add drained noodles, sesame oil, soy sauce, white pepper, diced meat, peas and green onions. Cook 5 minutes. Serve immediately. Makes 4 servings.

**Variation:** Add 1 cup coarsely chopped fresh spinach leaves in place of peas. Cook until leaves wilt.

# SPICY PORK WITH NOODLES

1/4 cup vegetable oil
1 lb. fresh mushrooms, sliced
1-1/2 lbs. pork cutlets
1-1/2 tbs. cornstarch
2 tbs. **each** soy sauce and dry sherry
3 tbs. vegetable oil
1 clove garlic, minced
6 green onions, thinly sliced
1 green pepper, coarsely chopped
1/2 tsp. Spice Islands Crushed Red Pepper (or to taste)
2 cups chicken broth
1 tsp. sesame oil
1 lb. cooked Chinese noodles or whole wheat spaghetti
1 pkg. (10 ozs.) frozen peas, cooked

Heat oil in large skillet. Saute mushrooms 4 to 5 minutes. Set aside. Slice pork into 1/4 x 1-inch matchsticks. Combine sliced pork with cornstarch, soy sauce and

sherry. Let stand 10 to 20 minutes. Heat oil in skillet or wok. When very hot add marinated pork, green onions, green pepper, garlic and red pepper. Stir constantly 3 to 4 minutes until pork is cooked. Remove meat from skillet and pour off any remaining oil. Stir in chicken broth. Bring to boil. Scrape brown bits from bottom of pan. Add mushrooms, pork, sesame oil and Chinese noodles. Cook a few minutes until all ingredients are hot. Stir in peas. Serve in a large bowl that has been warmed in oven. Makes 6 servings.

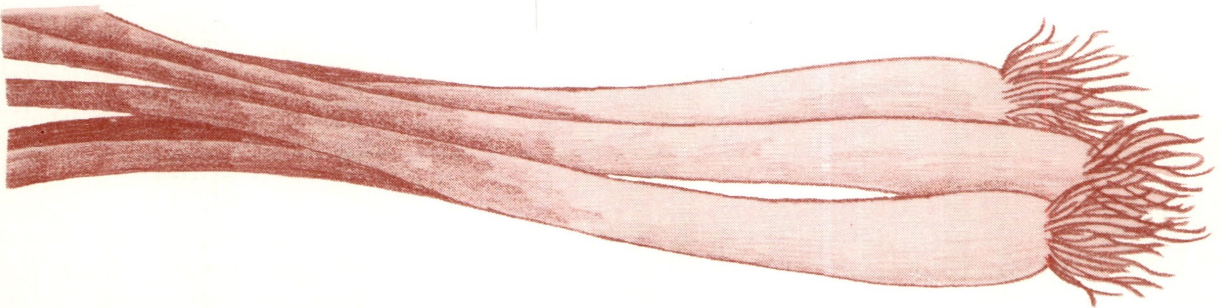

# PORK AND WATER CHESTNUT WON TON

Won ton can be deep fried for appetizers or simmered in rich broth for a hearty soup.

1/2 lb. ground pork
2 tsp. cornstarch
1 tbs. soy sauce
2 tsp. dry sherry
1 tsp. sesame oil
1 tbs. vegetable oil
salt and pepper
3 to 4 small fresh shrimp
1 egg white
4 green onions, finely chopped
6 water chestnuts, finely chopped
50 to 60 won ton wrappers

Combine pork, cornstarch, soy sauce, sherry and sesame oil. Mix well. Heat vegetable oil in medium skillet. Fry pork mixture 4 to 5 minutes, crumbling meat with a spatula while it cooks. Remove meat from skillet with a slotted spoon or drain in a sieve to remove as much fat as possible. Place meat in a small bowl. Add salt and pepper. Chop shrimp finely. Add to pork. Stir in egg white, green onions and water chestnuts. Mix well. Place 1 teaspoon filling in center of a won ton wrapper. (Keep unused wrappers covered with damp towel.) Moisten one-half of wrapper edge with water.

Fold over to form a triangle, pressing firmly around edges to seal. Moisten left tip of triangle. Bring the other tip around. Press tips together. Heat oil to 375°F. Fry won ton a few at a time until lightly browned. Drain on paper towels. Serve immediately.

## WON TON SOUP

4 cups chicken or beef broth
1 tbs. soy sauce
1/2 tsp. sesame oil
3 green onions finely chopped
1/2 tsp. pepper
20 to 25 filled won ton, uncooked (see page 64)
1/2 cup frozen peas
1/2 cup cooked diced carrot

Bring broth to boil. Add soy sauce, sesame oil, onions and pepper. Reduce heat to simmer and add won ton. Gently simmer uncovered 12 to 14 minutes. During the last 6 minutes of cooking add peas and carrots. Serve in soup bowls, ladling 5 or 6 won ton into each bowl with broth. Makes 4 servings.

# GREEN CHILE & CHEESE APPETIZERS

Won ton wrappers are used for this quick appetizer.

2 tbs. canned green chiles, seeded and finely chopped
1 cup grated Parmesan cheese
4 ozs. cream cheese
1 egg yolk
50 to 60 won ton wrappers
deep fat for frying

Combine chiles, Parmesan, cream cheese and egg yolk. Chill in refrigerator 20 to 30 minutes for easier handling. Fill wrappers one at a time. (Keep unused wrappers covered with a damp towel.) Place 1 teaspoon filling in center of won ton wrapper. Moisten one-half of wrapper edge with water. Fold over to form a triangle, pressing wrapper firmly around edges. Wet left tip of triangle with a little water. Bring the other tip around. Press together firmly. Heat oil to 375°F. Fry won ton a few at a time until very lightly browned. Drain on paper towels. Serve immediately with a mild taco sauce. Makes 50 to 60 appetizers.

# COCONUT AND PEANUT CRESCENTS

These are traditional Chinese New Year dessert won ton.

1/3 cup sweetened flaked coconut
1/3 cup chopped Spanish peanuts
2 tbs. sugar
30 to 35 round won ton wrappers
deep fat for frying

Combine coconut, peanuts and sugar. Make crescents one at a time. (Keep unused won ton wrappers covered with a damp towel.) Moisten top half edge of wrapper with a little water. Place 1 level teaspoon of coconut mixture in center of wrapper. Fold and bring edges together. Press firmly. Heat fat to 375°F. Fry crescents a few at a time until they are puffy and golden brown. Sprinkle with additional sugar and serve hot. Makes 30 to 35 crescents.

**Variation:** Almonds, cashews or pecans can be substituted for peanuts.

CLOVES
GINGER

# MORE PASTA FAVORITES

Casseroles and other main dishes using pasta are an excellent way to serve attractive delicious meals and still stay within the family food budget. Your favorite recipe will take on a new look with a different size or shape of pasta each time it's made.

Here are some other suggestions for using pasta in various ways:

Use cooked spirals, shells or broad noodles as a base for chili, goulash or stews.

Make a hearty pasta salad to serve with ham or a roast instead of potatoes, and serve Fettuccini Alfredo, Spaghetti Carbonara or macaroni with four different kinds of cheese for satisfying luncheon dishes.

Stuff jumbo shells with a chicken and nut filling and top with a Gruyere cheese and sherry sauce for an economical, make-ahead dish elegant enough for dinner guests.

Use egg noodles, Italian sausage and spinach as a novel and tasty stuffing for a roasting chicken or vegetables such as peppers, zucchini or tomatoes.

Make a Hungarian-style pasta dessert with nuts, applesauce and sour cream.

# FETTUCCINI ALFREDO

This is a classic recipe with a simple cream and cheese sauce for freshly cooked pasta.

8 ozs. uncooked fettuccini
2 tbs. butter
3/4 cup heavy cream
1/2 cup Parmesan cheese
nutmeg
salt
pepper

Cook fettuccini according to package directions. While pasta is cooking melt butter in a large skillet. Just before pasta is done, add cream and 1/4 cup cheese to skillet. Simmer over very low heat 4 to 5 minutes until sauce starts to thicken. Drain pasta well. Pour into skillet. Lift and stir to combine all ingredients and coat the pasta. Add remaining cheese, nutmeg, salt and generous amounts of pepper. Serve on warm plates. Makes 4 first course size servings.

# SPAGHETTI CARBONARA

Bacon, eggs and cream make a delicious pasta sauce.

1/2 lb. bacon
1 large onion, chopped
1/2 cup finely chopped parsley
2 eggs
3/4 cup Parmesan cheese
1/4 tsp. hot pepper flakes (optional)
1/2 cup heavy cream
1 lb. spaghetti
2 tbs. soft butter (for pasta)

Cut bacon into 1-inch pieces. Saute in skillet until crisp. Remove bacon pieces. Pour off all but 2 tablespoons bacon fat. Saute onion in bacon fat 3 to 4 minutes until soft. Combine parsley, eggs, Parmesan cheese, pepper flakes and cream in small mixing bowl. Cook spaghetti as directed. Drain well. Toss with butter in a warmed bowl. Quickly pour egg mixture over hot pasta and mix. Add bacon and onion. Toss to combine. Serve immediately. Makes 4 to 5 servings.

# FOUR-CHEESE MACARONI

1 pkg. (16 ozs.) macaroni
1 cup milk
1 cup cottage cheese
3 eggs
1 tsp. salt
1/8 tsp. white pepper
1/2 tsp. dry mustard
pinch nutmeg
1-1/3 cups grated sharp cheddar cheese
1-1/3 cups grated Swiss cheese
1/2 cup grated Parmesan cheese

Cook macaroni according to package directions. Drain well. In blender container place milk, cottage cheese, eggs, salt, pepper, mustard and nutmeg. Blend for a few seconds until well combined. Place one-third of cooked macaroni in a buttered casserole. Top with one-third each of the cheddar and Swiss cheeses. Add another layer of macaroni and another third of the cheese. Add remaining macaroni. Pour egg and

milk mixture over macaroni. Add remaining grated cheese. Sprinkle Parmesan over top. Bake in a 375°F. oven 20 minutes, or until hot and bubbly. Makes 6 servings.

**Variations:** Add 1 cup diced cooked ham and/or 1/2 cup diced canned green chiles between layers of macaroni as you are filling casserole.

Slice one onion into thin slices. Cut one green pepper into thin strips. Saute together in 2 tablespoons butter until soft. Place between layers of macaroni.

After pouring the egg-milk mixture over macaroni, make wells with back of tablespoon. Break one fresh egg into each well. Top with remaining grated cheese and Parmesan. Bake as directed.

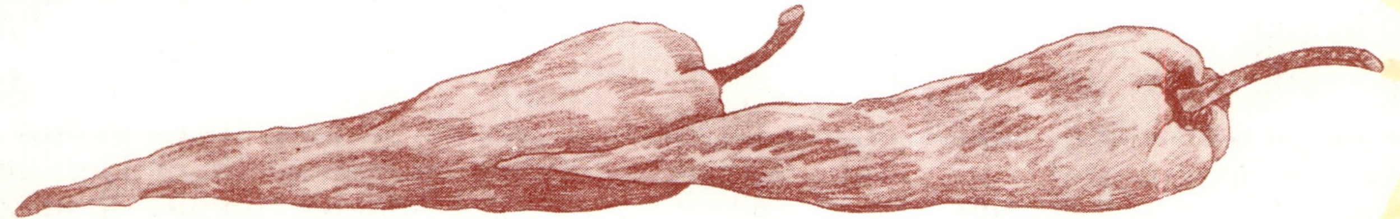

# OLD FASHIONED CHICKEN AND NOODLES

For a real old fashioned treat, make your own fresh noodles using the recipe on page 10. It's worth the extra effort.

1 stewing chicken (approx. 5 lbs.)
1 large carrot, sliced
1 large onion, sliced
1 stalk celery, sliced
1/2 cup dry white wine
2 qts. water
1/2 tsp. thyme
1 bay leaf
6 to 8 peppercorns
2 to 3 parsley sprigs
1 lb. fresh noodles, page 10
salt and pepper
2 tbs. butter
1/2 lb. fresh mushrooms, sliced
2 to 3 tbs. chopped pimientos

Cut chicken into pieces and place in large heavy pot with carrot, onion, celery, wine and water. Tie thyme, bay leaf, peppercorns and parsley in small piece of cheesecloth. Add to pot. Bring to boil, cover, and simmer over low heat 3 hours until chicken is tender. Remove chicken pieces from stock. When cool enough to handle remove chicken from bones and discard skin. Cut chicken into 3/4 to 1-inch cubes.

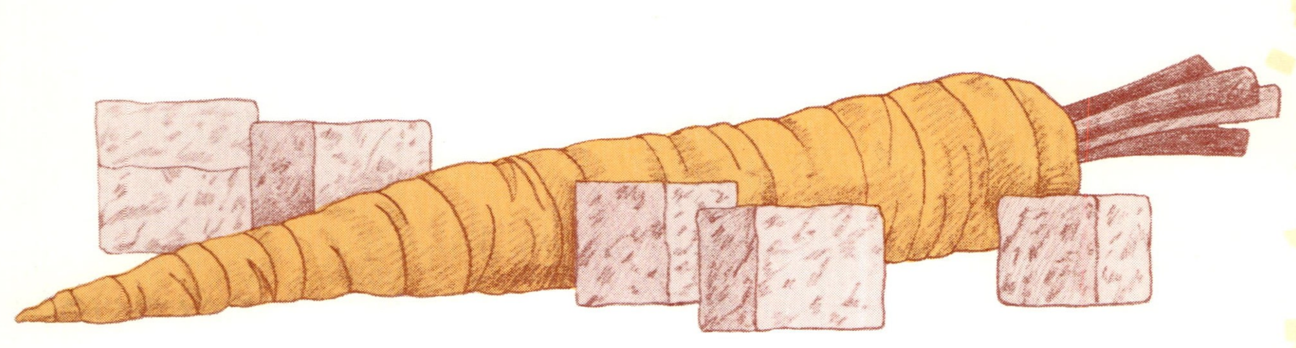

Refrigerate until you are ready to assemble dish. Strain stock through a coarse sieve. If possible, chill stock for several hours or overnight for easy removal of fat, or place in freezer until fat solidifies. Bring degreased chicken stock to boil. Cook uncovered over high heat until stock is reduced to 1 quart. Saute sliced mushrooms in butter 4 to 5 minutes. Set aside. Bring a large pot of water to boil. Cook fresh noodles 2 minutes to remove surface starch. Drain immediately and rinse. Bring chicken stock back to boil, add noodles, cubed chicken and mushrooms. Cook uncovered 8 to 10 minutes. Season with salt and pepper. Garnish with pimiento. Serve in soup plates. Makes 8 servings.

# WALNUT CHICKEN AND NOODLES

Crunchy walnuts add an interesting texture to this creamy chicken and noodle casserole.

7 tbs. butter
5 tbs. flour
3 cups chicken broth
1/3 cup dry sherry or white wine
1/2 tsp. paprika
1/2 tsp. salt
1/4 tsp. pepper
1/2 lb. fresh mushrooms, sliced
8 ozs. linguine or wide noodles
2 to 2-1/2 cups diced cooked chicken
1/2 cup coarsely chopped walnuts
Parmesan cheese

Melt 5 tablespoons butter in saucepan. Add flour. Cook, stirring 2 minutes. Gradually add chicken broth, sherry, paprika, salt and pepper. Cook, stirring constantly, until sauce thickens. Melt remaining butter in a medium skillet. Saute mushrooms 4 to 5 minutes. Cook noodles according to package directions. Drain well and place in buttered casserole. Add mushrooms, chicken and walnuts to casserole. Add sauce. Stir carefully to combine ingredients. Top with Parmesan cheese. Bake at 350°F. for 20 to 25 minutes until hot and bubbly. Makes 6 servings.

# EGG NOODLE STUFFING

Buttery egg noodles, spinach and sausage make a savory stuffing for two roasted chickens.

3 ozs. medium egg noodles
3 tbs. butter
3/4 cup finely diced celery
4 to 6 green onions, thinly sliced
1 medium clove garlic, minced
6 ozs. fresh spinach, coarsely chopped
3/4 cup diced cooked Italian or link sausages
1 tsp. salt
1/4 tsp. white pepper
2 (3 to 3-1/2 lbs. ea.) chickens

Cook noodles according to package directions. Melt butter in skillet. Saute celery, onions and garlic until soft but not brown. Stir in fresh spinach. Saute until wilted. Add diced sausage and drained noodles, salt and pepper. Mix well. Stuff chickens and tie with kitchen string. Roast on a rack in a 400°F. oven 1 hour. Place a small amount of water in bottom of roasting pan to keep juices from burning. Let rest 10 minutes before carving. Makes 4 to 6 servings.

# BAKED NOODLE PUDDING

Thin egg noodles are baked with applesauce, nuts, apricot jam and a sour cream topping for a Hungarian style dessert.

6 ozs. thin egg noodles
2 tbs. melted butter
3/4 cup applesauce
1/2 cup white raisins
1/2 cup finely chopped walnuts
1/4 cup brown sugar
1/4 tsp. cinnamon
1/3 cup apricot jam
3 eggs
1/4 cup sugar
1/2 cup sour cream
1/2 tsp. vanilla
dash nutmeg
pinch salt

Cook noodles according to directions. Drain well and place in mixing bowl. Immediately add melted butter, applesauce, raisins, walnuts, brown sugar and cinnamon. Pour into a buttered 1-1/2 quart souffle or baking dish. Spread jam over mixture. Beat remaining ingredients together until well combined. Pour over noodles. Bake uncovered in a 350°F. oven 40 minutes, until custard has puffed and pudding is firm and bubbling. Serve hot. Makes 6 servings.

# JUMBO SHELLS STUFFED WITH CHICKEN

Chicken-Nut Filling
Gruyere and Sherry Sauce, page 79
1/2 lb. jumbo shells
Parmesan cheese

Prepare filling and sauce. Cook shells as directed. Drain and rinse with cold water. Stuff shells with filling mixture using a small spoon. Place stuffed shells in buttered individual ramekins or a large casserole. Top with sauce. Sprinkle with Parmesan. Bake in 350°F. oven until heated through and bubbly. Place under broiler to lightly brown. Makes 4 servings.

## CHICKEN-NUT FILLING

1-1/2 cups cubed cooked chicken
1/2 cup coarsely chopped pecans
4 tbs. finely chopped parsley
1 egg
1 cup ricotta cheese
3 tbs. Parmesan cheese
1/2 tsp. salt
white pepper

Mix ingredients together well. Stuff cook shells with mixture.

## GRUYERE AND SHERRY SAUCE

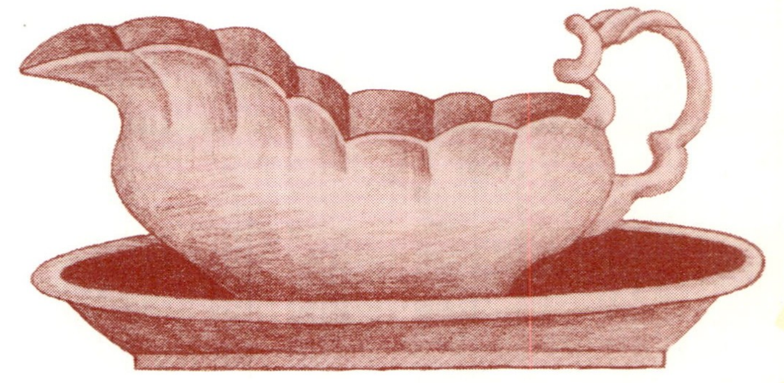

2 tbs. butter
1/4 cup minced shallots
3 tbs. flour
1-1/4 cups chicken broth
1/4 cup dry sherry
1/2 tsp. salt
white pepper
1/2 cup grated Gruyere cheese
1/4 cup whipping cream

Melt butter in small saucepan. Stir in shallots and cook one minute. Add flour and cook 2 minutes. Gradually add chicken broth and sherry. Cook over low heat stirring constantly until sauce thickens. Remove from heat. Add salt, pepper, grated cheese and cream. Spoon over filled shells.

# INDIAN CHICKEN AND MACARONI CASSEROLE

Boned chicken breasts with a subtle sour cream sauce make a delicious pasta casserole.

3 to 4 tbs. butter
4 chicken breast halves, boned
1/4 cup minced shallots or green onions
1 clove garlic, minced
2 tbs. flour
1-3/4 cups chicken stock
1 cup sour cream
1/4 tsp. cinnamon
1/4 tsp. ground coriander
1/4 tsp. cumin seed
1/2 tsp. ground cardamom
1/4 tsp. ground ginger
1/4 tsp. white pepper
1/2 tsp. salt
1 tsp. soy sauce
1/4 tsp. Tabasco
grated lemon rind
1-1/2 cups uncooked macaroni or tubetti
3 tbs. toasted sesame seeds

Melt butter in medium skillet. Saute chicken breasts over medium heat 3 to 4 minutes each side. Remove from skillet. Add shallots and garlic to pan. Cook a minute or two. Stir in flour and cook another minute. Add chicken stock. Cook, stirring, until

sauce thickens. Add sour cream, cinnamon, coriander, cumin, cardamom, ginger, pepper, salt, soy sauce, Tabasco and lemon rind. Mix well. Cook pasta according to package directions (approximately 10 minutes) in boiling water. Drain. Place in buttered casserole. Top with chicken breasts. Pour sour cream sauce over chicken. Sprinkle with sesame seeds. Bake in 350°F. oven 15 to 20 minutes until hot and bubbly. Makes 4 servings.

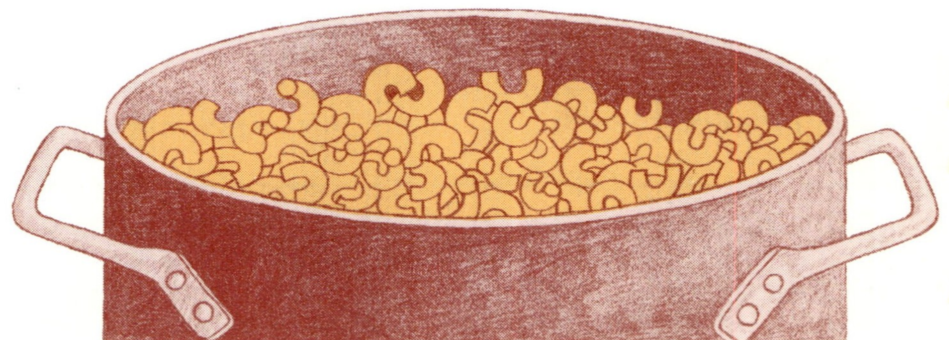

# ZUCCHINI AND PASTA CASSEROLE

Slices of crisp sauteed zucchini between layers of creamy pasta make a delicious casserole. Serve with sliced tomatoes and hot rolls.

4 medium zucchini
2 eggs
2 tbs. water
flour
1/4 to 1/3 cup olive oil
3 tbs. butter
6 small green onions, sliced
3 tbs. flour
2 cups milk
1/2 tsp. dry mustard
1 tsp. salt
1/4 tsp. white pepper
1 cup grated Swiss cheese
6 ozs. uncooked tubetti or salad macaroni
1/2 cup thinly sliced salami,
dried beef, or crumbled bacon
1/4 cup grated Parmesan cheese

Cut zucchini lengthwise into 1/4-inch slices. Beat eggs and water together. Dip zucchini first in flour then in beaten egg. Heat olive oil in a large skillet. Saute zucchini a few slices at a time. Drain on paper towels. Melt butter in small saucepan. Saute green onions 2 to 3 minutes until soft. Add 3 tablespoons flour. Cook, stirring, 2

minutes. Gradually add milk, mustard, salt and pepper. Cook over low heat, stirring constantly, until sauce thickens. Add cheese. Cook pasta according to package directions. Drain well. Reserve one fourth of the cheese sauce. Mix remaining sauce with cooked pasta. In 9 x 9-inch greased baking dish, place one layer of sauteed zucchini. Cover with one-half of the pasta and cheese sauce mixture. Sprinkle with one-half of the salami strips. Top with a layer of zucchini, the rest of the pasta mixture and salami and remaining zucchini. Pour reserved cheese sauce over top and sprinkle with Parmesan cheese. Bake uncovered in a 350°F. oven 15 to 20 minutes until hot and bubbly. Allow to stand 10 minutes after removing from oven. Serve in squares. Makes 4 to 5 servings.

**Variation:** Use 1/3 cup diced canned green chiles in addition to or in place of salami strips.

# MACARONI SALAD

This is a perfect picnic salad. For even better flavor, make it ahead and let it mellow in the refrigerator before serving.

1 cup uncooked salad macaroni
2 hard-cooked eggs, chopped
1 tbs. minced green onion
1/4 cup minced sweet pickle
1/4 cup finely diced celery
1 tbs. capers
1 cup cooked green peas
2 tbs. chopped pimiento

1/2 cup mayonnaise
2 tbs. pickle juice
1 tsp. prepared mustard
1/4 tsp. white pepper
1 tsp. salt
2 tbs. sour cream
1/2 tsp. chervil

Cook macaroni in boiling water for 12 minutes, or according to package directions. Drain and rinse with cold water. Drain well. Place in mixing bowl. Add chopped eggs, onion, pickle, celery, capers, peas and pimiento. Combine mayonnaise, pickle juice, mustard, pepper, salt, sour cream and chervil. Add to macaroni. Toss lightly with two forks to combine dressing and macaroni. Makes 4 to 6 servings.

# INDEX